Long after our own ashes have been scattered to the wind and our bones have turned to dust, it is entirely possible for whole pieces of ourselves, our histories, and the depth of our own unique existence to remain behind for our surviving loved ones to pore over and to ponder. It is these lasting remnants—the ones that we purposefully decide to preserve—that will offer the generations who come after us tangible evidence that we even existed at all, and that our years on this earth counted for something pleasing and positive.

—KRISTIN CLARK TAYLOR

The
FOREVER
BOX

Kristin Clark Taylor

BERKLEY BOOKS, NEW YORK

A BERKLEY BOOK
Published by the Penguin Group
Penguin Group (USA) Inc.
375 Hudson Street, New York, New York 10014, USA
Penguin Group (Canada), 90 Eglinton Avenue East, Suite 700, Toronto, Ontario M4P 2Y3, Canada
(a division of Pearson Penguin Canada Inc.)
Penguin Books Ltd., 80 Strand, London WC2R 0RL, England
Penguin Group Ireland, 25 St. Stephen's Green, Dublin 2, Ireland (a division of Penguin Books Ltd.)
Penguin Group (Australia), 250 Camberwell Road, Camberwell, Victoria 3124, Australia
(a division of Pearson Australia Group Pty. Ltd.)
Penguin Books India Pvt. Ltd., 11 Community Centre, Panchsheel Park, New Delhi—110 017, India
Penguin Group (NZ), 67 Apollo Drive, Rosedale, Auckland 0632, New Zealand
(a division of Pearson New Zealand Ltd.)
Penguin Books (South Africa) (Pty.) Ltd., 24 Sturdee Avenue, Rosebank, Johannesburg 2196, South Africa

Penguin Books Ltd., Registered Offices: 80 Strand, London WC2R 0RL, England

PRINTING HISTORY
Berkley hardcover edition / April 2011
Berkley trade paperback edition / April 2012

Berkley trade paperback ISBN: 978-0-425-24561-3

The Library of Congress has cataloged the Berkley hardcover edition as follows:

Taylor, Kristin Clark.
  The forever box / Kristin Clark Taylor.
     p.   cm.
  ISBN 978-0-425-24196-7 (hardback)
  1. Taylor, Kristin Clark—Childhood and youth.   2. African American women—Washington (DC)—
Biography.   3. Presidents—United States—Staff—Biography.   4. Public relations personnel—
Washington (DC)—Biography.   I. Title.
  E840.8.T39A3   2011
  973.928'092—dc22[B]   2010054244

PRINTED IN THE UNITED STATES OF AMERICA

10 9 8 7 6 5 4 3 2 1

This book describes the real experiences of real people. The author has disguised the identities of
some, and in some instances created composite characters, but none of these changes has affected the
truthfulness and accuracy of her story. Penguin is committed to publishing works of quality and
integrity. In that spirit, we are proud to offer this book to our readers; however, the story, the experiences, and the words are the author's alone.

For my sister
Noelle

Acknowledgments

Always, first and foremost, my prayer of gratitude to my heavenly Father for guiding my pen as I wrote and for speaking directly to my heart. It is through Him that all of my words flow; I am mightily fortified by His constant presence.

Profound thanks also to my six older siblings, Joann, Ingrid, Noelle, Donald, Tanya, and Nikki, for their boisterous love and for nurturing my spirit even as a young child. Mother and Daddy are smiling down on each of us, patting us gently on our heads because we've made them so very proud. How blessed I am to be "the baby" of this bunch, the happy little caboose at the end of our long familial train. Thank you for your shared memories, and for loving me as I wrote. My gratitude to each of you for creating the magic that was my childhood.

There are many miracles within the Berkley Publishing Group and I am grateful for having worked with several of them. My profound thanks to my editor, Denise Silvestro, for coaxing my words onto paper and for so gently pulling my childhood stories from the cobwebbed corners of my mind, straight into the bright and brilliant light of day. I know, beyond the shadow of a doubt, that our union was divinely inspired. My heart is so glad to have finally found you.

Also within the Berkley family, special thanks to Meredith Giordan, for assuring an orderly transition from manuscript to book, and to the two greatest publicists I know, Rosanne Romanello and Julia Fleischaker. To Leslie Gelbman, publisher of Berkley, as well as to the special folks within the larger publishing family of Penguin, my gratitude for providing the creative outlet I needed to share my stories.

To my wise and wonderful agent, Diane Freed: Can you feel the gratitude that's pouring from my heart? Thank you for your faith in me, and for guiding this book toward its true home. Thank you for folding me so lovingly into your literary embrace and for preserving the spirit of this project as it evolved. In you, I've found *two* blessings: an agent extraordinaire and a true friend as well.

The idea of one day writing about my Forever Box has been brewing in my soul for a bit. My longtime friend and fellow writer Laura Randolph was the first to nudge me forward with this project. Thank you, lovely Laura, for sprinkling your magic over my manuscript and for renewing my interest in *finally* giving birth to this little literary baby. You are extraordinary.

The Taylor family showered me, collectively and individually, with constant support and sustenance as I wrote. Thank you for rallying close. Special thanks to Steaven Coates Sr., the superb photographer, for handling the tiny treasures in my box with such admirable tenderness as he photographed them for this book, and for his keen and caring eye.

Of all the Taylor family, however, it is Lonnie Taylor who has molded and shaped my life in immeasurable ways. More than anyone, you have helped me evolve into the person I am today. Thank you for your support as I wrote and, from a larger perspective, for helping to create the biggest miracle of all: our two children, for without you they would not be.

How blessed I am to have so many wise and wonderful sister-friends in my life who kept me buoyant as I wrote. To my oldest friend in the world, Novellia "Cookie" Pounds, I thank you for the cherished childhood memories of playing Mother-May-I, making mud pies, and for the magical summer evenings we spent whispering together until the streetlights came on. I love you for always walking by faith and not by sight. Our late-night, long-distance prayer sessions kept me focused as I wrote. You are a miraculous and wondrous Woman of God.

My heart is happy and my spirit is glad to have been steered toward so many other special people who showered me with support as I wrote: Claud, Joann, Paige, Brant, and Claire Anderson; Fred and Bryna Berman; Marga Bushara; Donald, Anthony, and Michelle Clark; Valerie Cooley-Elliot; Kathleen Farrell; Kianna Ferguson; Susan Friedman; Karen Gaddis; Carlos and Linda Jones; Andre Latham; LaRita Lynch; Charlie Miles; Elena Motaynep; Vickie West; and everyone at Elite. Tender kisses also to my special, quiet friends who never judge but always love; thank you for accepting me simply for who I am.

Finally, and most important, it is my two children, Lonnie Paul and Mary Elizabeth, who stoke the fire in my heart. That you both came *through me* on your way into this world is a miracle of such magnitude that it takes my breath away. It fills my soul with comfort and gladness to know that, long after I leave this earthly place, the two of you will step forward to become the careful keepers of our familial flame. You'll carry the torch and light the light. Because you exist, I am certain that my life has not been lived in vain. Because you exist, I am certain that our legacy will live on . . . which is about as close to the comforting, concentric concept of *forever* as I really need to get.

Contents

INTRODUCTION

———— ❧ ————

CEDAR.

The sharp, pungent smell of its woody fragrance makes my soul smile. When I inhale deeply, I can actually feel the weight of its dusky scent lingering lightly in the recesses of my memory. Its aroma brings back the blustery feel of a crisp winter day; barren oak trees standing tall, their branches stretching like old, arthritic fingers, reaching higher and higher to scrape the sky.

The smell of cedar steers me directly toward countless age-old mental snapshots from my past—memories and mementos that are now carefully stored away within the depths of a handsome, heavy cedar repository, which I call my Forever Box. In my box are precious, tangible pieces of my past that can be touched and turned around in my own hands whenever I please: a yellowed newspaper article about a family member now long gone, the tiny clay elephant my daughter made for me when she was a mere toddler, love notes and ribbons and many things magical—all of them steeped in the pleasing and powerful scent of cedar.

A quick whiff will magically re-create an isolated memory from my childhood. Suddenly, I am transported to a golden, sun-splashed fall afternoon, twirling, twirling in our backyard, my thin brown arms outstretched and my face turned upwards toward the sky.

Other cedar-scented memories abound. The earliest is not even one of my own, but was told to me by my brother and five sisters. Early in my infancy, so it was said, my mother would swaddle me in my Cinderella pink baby blanket and carry me downstairs so that the two of us could stay close while she wrote. Since we couldn't afford the luxury of an upstairs crib *and* a downstairs crib, Mother simply improvised and made do with what she had—an instinctive, protective, universal skill shared by mothers everywhere.

Removing a wide, cedar-lined drawer from their bedroom bureau, Daddy would dutifully carry the drawer downstairs and place it in a corner in our living room. Mother, holding me in a squirming bundle, would lean over to gently, lovingly, place me inside. There I'd lie while she wrote, her baby girl (the youngest of seven), swaddled and secure inside the cedar drawer, joyous beyond belief from simply listening to the happy, hollowed-out *tap-tap-tapping* sounds of Mother working away on her Underwood typewriter. So perhaps it is as early as then, when I was weeks old, that the smell of cedar first permeated my soul.

Today, the pungent aroma of cedar helps solidify my own sense of stability and continuity. It reminds me of that vision from my infancy, as told to me by my siblings, of Mother sitting primly at our olive-green card table in the corner of the living room, typing furiously, leaning down into my makeshift cedar "crib-drawer" every now and then to kiss me on my forehead while I napped. (Mother's old Underwood typewriter, still bulky and beautiful, sits in my home library today, shrouded in her heavenly presence, many of its keys well-worn from the constant pressure of her slender fingers so many decades ago.)

There are other memories, too, which surface the second I open the lid of my Forever Box and touch one of the treasures inside. My imagination might pick me up and swing me straight back to my first day of kindergarten. I remember with startling clarity the smell of Elmer's Glue swimming around my head and the Dance of the Butterflies fluttering deep down in the pit of my stomach, and how my heart yearned so desperately for Mother to come and whisk me back to the safety of our home.

The beauty of positive, pleasing memories is that *every*

one of us can call them up, at will. But it takes time. Practice. Discipline. Who among us, for instance, can ever forget their first day of school—what we wore, where we sat, how we felt? With very little effort and a great deal of joy, I am back there again, at the first day. The open, sunny classroom. The biting, brilliant feeling of excitement that showered over my little shoulders as I sat with my classmates at the hexagonal-shaped art table. The mild nervousness that moved around in my little spirit as I sat at that table, preparing to embark on my first art project. Yes, I can remember quite clearly how each one of us sat ramrod-straight, intent and focused on the art assignment we'd just received from our teacher (which involved drawing various shapes onto colored construction paper). And if I sit still long enough, I can even conjure up my teacher's essence; her rosebud mouth (which reminded me of a knot in a balloon), her sensible brown lace-up shoes, and the way her bracelets tinkled softly when she passed around more construction paper or put out more glue.

I recall the details. Sitting at that art table all decked out in my finest first-day-of-school red plaid jumper, passionately praying that the flaxen-haired beauty sitting beside me wouldn't reach right over and snatch the last red crayon before I could swipe it for myself. How in the world was I to draw an apple for Mother if all the red crayons had already been taken?

And in the end, it hadn't really mattered that I'd had to

use a purple crayon to draw my apple (alas, all the red crayons had been taken). Nor did it matter that my coloring skills were untidy and more than a little wild—or that some of my strokes were so hard they tore clean through the paper.

What *did* matter way, way back then (and still counts for so much today) is that Mother loved my purple apple simply because I'd made it with my own hands—and because I'd made it for *her.* She loved it so much she taped it to our kitchen wall for all to admire—and eventually, she carefully packed her precious piece of art into her own Forever Box, for successive generations to admire and appreciate.

Today, decades after her death, I still have that purple apple, and it sits nestled safely in the lower-left-hand corner of my Forever Box. Why? Because Mother had the presence of mind, even back then, to save it so that I would have it for *today.* She purposefully preserved that piece of our past— which I, in turn, have preserved for my own children, and which they will eventually share with their own progeny.

Decades later, my drawing remains perfectly intact. Most of the paste still adheres. My name is still clearly scrawled in that careful, kindergarten penmanship, along the lower-right-hand corner of the paper. And at any time of the day or night, when my adult son or daughter pulls open the heavy lid of my Forever Box, they can feel for themselves the wild, waxy crayon tracks that their mother drew all those many years ago. (I'd drawn Daddy a similar picture during my first day in nursery school, but at least *that* time I'd been lucky enough to get to the red crayon first!)

It fills my soul with gladness that my children are so easily able to return with me to those precious memories from the past.

Memories of their mother in her brand-new jumper on the first day of school.

Memories of the powerful, pungent smell of cedar on a crisp, wintry day.

Memories of yesterday, today, and forever.

ᏭᎦ

THE magic that occurs whenever I open my Forever Box is mesmerizing; almost miraculous. When I reach down into its depths to withdraw a precious trinket, I am transported to a past that is rich in color and pulsating with the power of yesterday.

Throughout most of this book, I am seven years old again, growing up in Detroit during the 1960s, a powerful, pent-up time when Motown crackled with culture, color, and finger-snapping energy.

Yes, indeed, my childhood was wondrous. I was happy. Safe. Surrounded by love and laughter. A skinny-legged, little golden-brown girl with fuzzy pigtails and a penchant for making friends who were decades older than me.

These elderly women are also "the special ones" I celebrate

within the pages of my book, along with the principles they instilled in my spirit and the life lessons they passed along, which will live on, quite literally, forever. I celebrate their collective stories, and the extraordinary tales of their own youth, as well as the trinkets they so generously shared with me (which are now safely preserved in my Forever Box) before they departed this earth. I celebrate the friendships we forged and the love that bounced between and within us every time we were together—infinite, otherworldly, everlasting love, which neither the passage of time nor the inevitability of death can erase.

&

In the crafting of this book, I also hope to offer a precious peek at some of the treasures so carefully stored inside my Forever Box. Every photo shown within these pages is a piece that actually lives within the cedar box's darkened recesses: antique lace and crocheted doilies, beaded bags, and favorite childhood books. A heartbreakingly beautiful teacup and saucer set, given to me when I was a child, by an elderly neighbor-friend one rainy, summer afternoon, just after we'd finished praying together in her parlor. The christening gown worn by myself and all six of my siblings at different times during our infancy, on that special day when each of us took our first spiritual steps toward our living, loving God.

But it is not solely the *stuff* in my Forever Box that I celebrate.

Far from it.

This is a clamorous, clanging celebration of what can happen when we—all of us—actively, mindfully, decide to preserve the most positive pieces of our past and pass them down to the generations who will follow in our footsteps long after we've taken our last breath.

I am a memory-maker, a keeper of keepsakes. And within these pages, I issue to you a personal invitation: Learn how to mindfully appreciate the power of preservation. Experience the magic that begins the moment you begin preserving the special trinkets and treasures from your personal past. Become a memory-maker in your own right.

Plucking from the past deepens my spirit and connects me more directly to the wondrous, fast-moving world around me. Whether it's my mason jar filled with antique buttons or, more elaborately, a few of the dried red roses preserved from the day of my mother's funeral, in those final moments before I uttered to her my last good-bye, I've learned to come as close to forever as I can get. How? By rustling up yesterday's sounds and images so they can become a comfortable, conscious part of my daily life.

Long after our own ashes have been scattered to the wind and our bones have turned to dust, it is entirely possible for whole pieces of ourselves—our histories and the depth of our own unique existence—to remain behind for our surviving loved ones to pore over and to ponder. It is these lasting remnants—the ones we purposefully decide to preserve—that offer the generations who will come after us tangible evidence that we even existed at all, and that our years on this earth counted for something positive and pleasing.

I hope that my stories—real-life, childhood vignettes that unfold over the course of several rain-soaked summer days—will slow you down and lift you up. In a few instances, my childhood recollections may be a bit murky, the mental images shadowed and cobwebbed. But what remains as clear as a summer day is the laughter and love that permeated my soul on those four magical days. I hope that before we begin our journey you'll close your laptops and disconnect all things electronic so that we can travel back to those slow, languid days of yesterday—to the stories that spring from the purest parts of my past.

The first story is about Mother, an elegant, golden wisp of a woman whose lingering spirit will cover me, always, in gladness, glory, and eternal love.

Sweet Mother, resplendent in her elegant church hat.

Kristin Clark Taylor

CHURCH HAT

⸎

I WATCHED HER CLOSELY as she slept.

As far as I could tell, her breathing was normal, but still, I was worried. I leaned in closer, peering for additional proof that my sweet mother was alive, beyond the shadow of a doubt. The rise and fall of her chest was simply not enough to convince me, 171 percent, that she was still with me in the land of the living. So, as gently as I possibly could, I reached over toward her slender, bronze-brown wrist and felt for a pulse. How much could a seven-year-old girl actually know about the normalcy of her mother's pulse? Yet still, I tried, just like I'd seen it done on *Dr. Kildare*. After a second or two, I felt a soft throbbing. She was alive for sure. Mother hadn't left me alone on this earth after all. She was only enjoying a rare and much-deserved afternoon nap on our living room sofa.

Mother and Daddy were decidedly, deliciously, devoted to raising their seven children in the bright light of love, laughter, and spiritual solidity. There was nothing more important to the two of them than bringing us up to know that we were loved—and boy, did we know it. They also taught us to cling to several beliefs that remain, to this day, ingrained in our spirits. The first, we were to worship our heavenly Father with all our hearts, minds, and souls because we were His children, and He was our gentle Savior. The second, we were to treat others as we ourselves expected to be treated; that is, with unconditional love, kindness, compassion, and respect. And the third, we were to always, *always* be mindful of the fact that both of them loved us with a fiery, ferocious intensity. These powerful beliefs and principles bounced and swirled happily around us when we were all growing up. Yes indeed, all seven of us—my brother, my five sisters, and I—knew, with startling clarity, that we were well loved. Such comforting knowledge allowed us to walk with a certain swagger that would bounce us up to the tips of our toes. It instilled in us a powerful spunk and verve, as well as a conscious bond with and awareness of God Himself. We knew, sure as shooting, that God was good—because Anybody who would put two people like Mother and Daddy on His good, green earth must be hugely and heavenly Supreme.

On this particular afternoon, though—even at the tender age of seven-going-on-eight—I was still keenly aware that I shouldn't have been nitpicking at Mother while she rested. So why did my fingers keep brushing her cheek and why was I trying so valiantly, what with the pulse-taking and all, to assure myself that she was still alive? *Because I simply couldn't help myself. I wanted her awake.* I wanted her eyes to flutter open, find their focus, and rest their gentle gaze directly and solely on me. I needed to feel the pounding of her heart strongly enough through her pretty polka-dot sundress so that I could match it with my own heart rhythms. I adored my mama in great, gulping doses—so much so that I actually missed her while she slept.

This particular afternoon, as summer thunder rumbled far off in the distance, Mother's nap seemed to have transported her to another place entirely. As I continued to study her, it gradually occurred to me that she was in the midst of a delicious dream. She smiled softly, eyes still closed. I wanted to kick myself or maybe bite my own tongue because I was so frustrated over our separation. I was powerless. Her smile told me she was in the clutches of pleasant slumber— maybe she was lying on a white, sandy beach with palm trees swaying in a balmy breeze; or dreaming my favorite fantasy: lying suspended in midair, on top of a billowing, fast-moving cloud. Suffering succotash! I was growing madder by the minute—not at her, but at myself for not being able to reach her, wherever she was. I thought of doing something naughty—spitting on our living room carpet or ripping the "Do Not Remove" label from one of the sofa cushions—as a cheap tactic to finally wake her up and get her attention. But I didn't. I couldn't. And still she slept. Out like a light. Her left cheek lay flat against the knobby arm of the sofa and her legs stretched out gracefully, like two golden parentheses, along the sofa's length.

Finally, I turned to God Himself.

Lifting my face upward toward the ceiling, I prayed a hopeful prayer: *Please wake Mother up soon, God, so that we can laugh and talk and laugh some more. And if You can, while you're at it, please wake her up before anyone else gets home so that we can have precious personal minutes to ourselves.*

Nothing.

But then, all of a sudden, I got another idea about how best to wake Mother up. The eyelid-blowing test! Why in the world hadn't I thought of that before? The eyelid-blowing test, in my mind, was the final litmus test that could really, truly gauge if someone was either alive (and just sleeping) or dead as a doornail. So I leaned in close yet again and blew gently onto her closed eyelids. Her eyelashes fluttered slightly, but she quickly seemed to settle back into her dream world. Propelled by something I couldn't identify—something deep inside me, which I now realize was the powerful pull of "Mother-love"—I blew yet *again*. This time, I used much more sudden, forceful puffs, just to make sure I'd finally gotten her attention. I needed my heart to get on the same page as my head. I needed to make sure my mama was alive.

It worked! Sort of.

Mother sighed softly, murmuring something about raisin oatmeal and tigers in the attic, then she shifted her position slightly more toward me; that beautiful, brown face of hers now partially shadowed by the late afternoon sun-and-cloud combination of that strange-weather day.

I had her now. It was time to rock and roll.

"Ma? You awake?" I whispered hotly into her ear.

The sound of my voice was so close it must have felt moist. I was being completely irrational. How could she be awake when I was watching her *sleep*? As I spoke, I could hear my own seven-year-old voice cracking in quiet desperation. I wanted my mama.

Instinctively, her right arm reached out for me and encircled my tiny waist, drawing me in closer. She was waking slowly, swimming back up toward the surface of consciousness, but still being cuddled in the arms of a pleasant summer-afternoon thunderstorm dream.

Her touch touched me directly. I dropped my small face straight down into the graceful, soapy-smelling curve of her neck. Safe. Secure. Even my waist was elated, because Mother was touching it. At that moment, I knew exactly where I needed to be. *Not* outside jumping double Dutch between the raindrops with my friends, or splashing around in my red rubber rain boots out back. No sirree. I was with Mother. Nowhere else and no one else existed in the world.

"Ma? I have to ask you something *important*," I whispered urgently, lying through my little white Chiclet teeth.

Her beautiful skin shone reddish-brown, the color of a shiny copper penny. I noticed the startling highlights in her complexion, so beautiful I could have scooped them up with my hands, like golden nuggets. What on earth was I going to ask her when she fully came to? When the raisin oatmeal or tigers in the attic or whatever else she was dreaming about finally fluttered away and I was left standing there, looking expectant and immature and demanding? I knew full well I had no specific question on—or in—my mind. All I wanted her to do was come back from her dream and send her brilliant, sun-splashed smile bouncing directly toward me.

"Yes, baby?" she hummed. "What's going on in that little head of yours? What question do you have for your mama that is just so important?"

I could feel her willfully trying to pull herself out of sleep, bless her dutiful heart. She was the best of mothers to her children *even while she slept*. She hadn't gotten mad or even a little bit salty when I'd blown on her eyelids or pulled at her wrist. (If someone had bothered me like that while I slept, I probably would have pinched the soft flesh under their arm.)

But not Mother. Somehow, she knew I needed her.

I don't know much, but I do know this: *All* mothers can sense, in the deepest part of their souls, the precise moment when their child needs them. They just can. Mother knew I needed her then. I still need her today.

"What's on your mind, Beauty?" she asked again, more alert this time. A slow smile danced a lazy samba across her face as she finally found and met my gaze. She sat up and reached for me again, drawing me to her, leaning over toward me to plant a sweet, brown Hershey-chocolate mother-kiss smack in the middle of my forehead. I loved her as much as I loved God and Jesus and peanut M&M's; a strong, strange love that is not of this world at all, but from some other place I've never seen, visited, or even read about in our Encyclopedia Brittanica.

She was the most beautiful, brilliant woman I'd ever seen. Skin the color of soft caramel candy. High cheekbones shaped like little mountains. Eyelashes of mink. Hands small and birdlike, prominently veined like my grandmother's, and like mine. A laugh that tinkled like fine crystal; her laughter never guffawed or banged around the room like a noisy brass band.

By anybody's standards (not just my own), Mother was breathtaking. Her physical beauty attracted attention. In her younger days, as a way to offset the cost of her college tuition, she'd worked once in a while as a professional model, so her image popped up in public from time to time. Newspapers published photos of her with captions underneath describing her as a rare jewel of unparalleled beauty. I'm sure such attention embarrassed my humble mother. To her, vanity was a bad habit; unseemly and off-putting. She and Daddy never tolerated it from any of their children.

The *Pittsburgh Courier* ran a front-page article about her, with a banner headline reading, "Brown Venus Is Carnegie Tech Model," and then the subhead, "Has Posed at Yale,

Mary Elizabeth Clark
COURTESY OF THE AUTHOR

Harvard." The article itself showered Mother with praise and affection, and when I actually read it for myself a few years later, I was actually taken aback, knocked slightly off balance.

The accompanying photo revealed a profile that was unmistakable, the posture intimately familiar. There she stood, probably in her late teens or early twenties, gloriously draped in a dark velvet sheath that flowed off her bare shoulders and rested in a graceful pool at her feet. Seeing this "other" side of Mother stirred my spirit in a new and intense way; it was the first time I'd seen her as anything other than a devoted wife, the loving mother of seven children, and a professional career woman we were all proud of. Heck; that she even *had* a life before us—and a thriving, exciting, fairly glamorous life at that—seemed incongruous and illogical. Gazing at the newspaper and magazine articles, my heart raced. Was this woman really Mother—or just some wise guy trying to pull a prank on me? How was it that she had not only existed but thrived in a world without us? How was it possible that someone had dubbed her "Brown Venus" before even I had dubbed her "Mother?"

It almost didn't fit. But this much was clear: Whoever wrote that headline had been right on target: Mother was, indeed, a "Brown Venus." Both the article and the photos were mesmerizing.

There she stood in a graceful, languid pose, small, perfect

hands held as delicately as a china doll's. Surrounding her in a small circle were a handful of serious artists, all sitting on stools with their canvases and easels in front of them, all obviously concentrating very hard on trying to capture her beauty for all time.

There were other articles as well. "Sepia Siren," one newspaper called her. "The world's most perfect face and figure." (It is said that a sculpture still stands of her today in one of the exclusive private boarding schools in Michigan.) She was absolutely captivating. That this wonderful, wise woman *belonged to me* was a gift that simply took my breath away.

On this particular afternoon, though, I wasn't thinking about modeling or magazines or art students sitting on stools. I was trying to figure out how I was going to fully engage her attention, now that she seemed to be awake. Part of me felt guilty for having pestered her so relentlessly. But mostly I felt happy because that very same pestering had finally paid off: She was awake and she was reaching out to pull me closer and—for the moment, anyway—she belonged exclusively to me!

Rare as it was, the house was almost empty. The only ones home were my older sister Noelle, who was upstairs studying in her bedroom; and our cat, Kaboodle, who slinkslithered around the legs of our living room table.

I still had to come up with a question, though. Nothing came to me.

"What *is* it, sweetheart?" Mother asked, beginning to sense, incorrectly, that I might be sick or in need of a fever check (the cool flat of her hand against my forehead used to make me happy to be sick).

"Is something bothering my Beauty?" (She called me this often, but I noticed she used it mostly when we were by ourselves. Why? Because I am certain, even way back then, that she was sending me a private message. At least twice a week, she'd read to me from Anna Sewell's heartbreaking but endearing novel, *Black Beauty*; a story of how this beautiful black horse suffered through many trials and travails, yet still emerged victorious—"on the *good* side of bad," as Mother used to like to say. In her own way, especially during those racially charged years of the mid-'60s, she was instilling in me the wonderfully immutable fact that I was indeed *black* and I was indeed *beautiful*—a message every black child needed to hear, especially growing up during those tumultuous years. By selecting this particular book, and reading it to me regularly, Mother was purposefully and gracefully showering me with a sense of racial pride and heightened self-esteem. Sure, the book was about a horse. But its underlying message—and even its title—cemented within me a powerful place of contentment and a more stabilized sense of self-awareness.

She was fully awake now and looking expectant. After a minute or two, she sat up.

My stomach felt rumbly. Worry and guilt rose up into my throat like bile. One thing Mother didn't abide by in any of her seven children was lying. And lying was exactly what I'd done when I told her I had an "important" question to ask. My longing for her attention at any cost was beginning to backfire and trip all over itself with frightening speed, and even worse, I think it was beginning to dawn on her, too. Her youngest child, her baby girl, her Black Beauty, had simply been fibbing to get a little attention.

I eased down onto the sofa and stretched out my short body so that my head was smack dab in the middle of her warm lap. We fit together on our sofa perfectly. A summer breeze blew, causing the metal blinds to clatter lightly at the open window above us. From my lying-down position, I gazed up through the open blinds and spied a piece of the sky; clouds hanging low with moisture and growing darker by the minute. I inhaled deeply, pulling in her magnificent mother-smells and the heavy, newly wet earth smells from outside, and I thought to myself, *This must be what heaven is like*. My stomach was still a-rumbling with worry, though. And the fact that Mother was now fully awake and catching on to my fib made me temporarily redefine my notion of heaven—because there was no way in the world heaven would have opened its Pearly Gates to let in lying, manipulative seven-year-old girls. Of this I was certain.

Suddenly, I had an idea. God and Jesus and Captain

Kangaroo dropped it straight into my brain as a little gift. I had it! A legitimate reason for having awakened Mother!

"Tell me about the time you went downtown to buy yourself that hat for church," I demanded as demurely as I could.

I wanted to hear her voice, to feel the warmth of her body and the rhythm of her chest as she spoke. I needed the drama of her long-ago, real-life story to wrap itself around my narrow shoulders like a sheer summer garment, and Mother was the only one to satisfy that need. It was a story I'd heard at least a hundred times before, but somehow it never grew old. Even Kaboodle stopped slinking around and adopted a dignified-looking, sphinx-like position under the table, ears perked up ramrod straight, ready to actually listen—rare, indeed, given the finicky nature of the feline. Thunder rumbled again, this time closer. The metal blinds continued their clattering, and upstairs, a sudden breeze slammed the bathroom door shut. Mother touched my cheek lightly with the back of her hand. My soul smiled.

"You're sure you're not tired of this story by now, sweetheart?" she asked in mock amazement.

She knew in her heart that I would never tire of it, and I knew in my own that she never *wanted* me to. It was an experience that we simply could not let breathe its last breath, even if Mother herself would—and did—breathe hers.

"I'll never be tired of the church hat story, Ma. *Never.*"

I wasn't lying then. Only the truth stirred around in my heart.

"Okay, then, you got it," she said in agreement. Absently, she stroked my bare arms. *Thankyouthankyouthankyou*, every hair follicle and skin cell on my forearms whispered softly, silently up into her face. *Thank you for your touch.*

"You know how Mommy likes to dress up real nice and pretty for church, right?" she asked, setting the story up.

I nodded yes before she could even finish the question, for we both knew it was rhetorical. It was *always* the question she started with. I nodded again, blinded by the protective power of her proximity. She did indeed get all gussied up and fancy for church. She was right about that part. Every Sunday, she and Daddy would take charge of the spiritual assembly line of preparing six girls, one boy, and themselves for the eleven o'clock service. Because there were nine of us altogether, plentiful supplies were required, which is why we had a huge cardboard box that was filled to the brim with a variety of Sunday-go-to-meeting paraphernalia. Although somewhat jumbled, the box always seemed to hold whatever we needed: White church gloves in various sizes. Velvet headbands. Knee socks and half-slips. Lacy anklets. Patent leather pocketbooks. And what wasn't in the box could usually be found on our bathroom counter (which was usually neat but always cluttered): a barrage of bobby pins, barrettes, Dixie Peach hair oil, Dippity-do hair gel, AquaNet

Hairspray, VO5, pink sponge curlers and, for the eldest sisters, tubes and tubes of Maybelline mascara. (My brother and father always seemed a bit more organized; there were only so many belts, ties, and crisply-starched handkerchiefs two men could actually need.)

When it was time for church, our collective excitement and expectation ricocheted off every wall. A current of spiritual electricity hummed through the house.

A big day in the Clark household, Sundays. People got pretty and God stepped in close.

We all looked good, the nine of us, and we filled up our very own pew (second from the front, on the left side of the church if you're facing the pulpit).

But Mother looked the best.

"Well, long before you were born, Beauty, I took the bus downtown to buy myself a new church hat. Lord knows I needed a new one, and I'd had my eye on a pretty sharp one for quite some time. I'd saved a little extra money, and I was determined to get that hat! If it was the last thing I did, your mother was going to buy that charming church hat."

Silence. I was already lost in her loving, literary presence. I could barely speak or even breathe. Every image Mother painted as she spoke sprang to life, jumping out from behind the darkened nooks and crannies of my little mind like miniature, friendly-faced ghosts.

As I lay there looking up at her face, I visualized Mother,

for the thousandth time, as a much younger woman, standing patiently at the corner bus stop in the searing heat, picking delicately through her small, beaded change purse for
the exact bus fare. Although she never said that it was the
law back then for black people to sit at the back of the bus—
even a glorious, gold-dusted woman like Mother simply on
her way downtown to buy a church hat—I already sensed as
much. I also vaguely wondered why Daddy hadn't just
driven her downtown. (In Detroit, the venerable Motor City,
every family owned a car, and for this reason, Mother drove
only rarely. Daddy did all the driving. I finally concluded
that, on this particular day, Daddy must have been at work.)

She continued, still stroking my happy arms.

"It was a Saturday afternoon, and my, was that bus
crowded!" Mother remembered, a hint of sadness in her
smile.

I visualized the perspiring passengers and the oppressive
heaviness of heat and maybe even hatred rolling outward
from their bodies like waves. There'd be a blond-haired,
middle-aged man seated in the front of the bus, maybe on
his way to the racetrack, hoping and praying his lucky horse
would come in. Or the red-haired, freckled-faced housewife
riding in from Farmington Hills, eager to make it downtown, too, to nab that set of butcher-block knives she'd
heard were only on sale until Monday—but in my imagination, both of *them* sat at the front of the bus.

I even visualized the bus driver, with his wide, bountiful butt melting miserably over the sides of his raised platform driver seat, his hardened, beady eyes like tiny raisins looking impatiently at the beautiful bronze woman who was my mother. I could almost feel the bus driver's impatience toward Mother as she made her way up the bus steps. And there, standing like tall but wilting ears of corn in a choked cluster at the back, stood the black people. Hot. Silent. Stoic.

Because of Mother's amazing grace and gentle humility, it was always difficult for me to visualize exactly where or how she herself fit into that crowded cornfield, but I knew she must have made her way to the back of that bus, simply because it was expected—and I bet you dollars to doughnuts she probably did it without rancor, resentment, or riled-up feelings of white-hot hatred. She was on a mission. She was going to board that bus and get downtown to buy that hat if it was the last thing she did.

"What happened when you finally got there, Ma?" I asked, trance-like.

We were dancing a dance together, Ma and me. She was leading, and I was blissfully following her every step.

"Well, I pulled that cord hard, because I was coming to my stop. It seemed as though that entire bus wanted to get off at that stop with me!" *But the black folks had to get off last. You had to wait, Ma, for all the other ladies—and even all the other men—to get off before you. And even then, you probably had to exit through the back. All that indignity just for a pretty church hat.*

"Let me tell you, Beauty; that store was as crowded as I've ever seen it!" she exclaimed softly, shaking her head at the very memory. Her long, slender fingers picked a fleck of lint from my dress, and then patted my arm gently.

"But I knew exactly where I was going, believe me when I tell you I did, Krissy baby. Nothing could have stopped me that day. Plus, I'd called several days ahead and spoken to a very nice saleslady. Each time I called to check on whether my hat was still there, the saleslady smiled through her voice and promised me that it was."

Pushing her voice up an octave and expertly adopting the voice of a somewhat snooty saleslady, Mother imitated the clerk:

"'Yes, ma'am, it's here, all right. I'm looking right at it!'"

Mother was great when it came to imitating people. She was on a roll and continued imitating the saleslady.

Mother threw her head back gently and laughed, the sound tinkling like the wind chimes hanging under our porch in the backyard.

(I loved our backyard, with my swing set back near the tomato plants and the small patch of lily of the valley near our wire fence. I even had a playhouse, which sat on a small patch of grass just beside our back porch, strong and real and sturdy as a poplar—and oh, what a playhouse it was! It wasn't plastic like Barbie's and it was much, *much* bigger than the houses you could make with Lincoln Logs or LEGOs. This was a *life-size* house—big enough for me and my best friend, Cookie, to actually stand up in!)

But here's the real reason my house was as precious to me as a boxful of Sugar Daddys and cinnamon sticks: Daddy built it just for me, with his own two hands. Granted, it was a tad ramshackle, and it did lean a tiny bit to the right, but he'd made it for *me*—and I loved him for it. Cookie and I even managed to squeeze in a tiny table and a couple of rickety three-legged stools, which afforded us countless imaginary tea parties, with real-life mud pies that we'd make with our own hands—mixing dirt and water, then pouring the concoction into one or two of my mother's aluminum pie tins.

Sure, Daddy built my house using worn, irregular pieces of warped wood, which I think came from the alley, but my humble abode had a real window with curtains and a real door with a real doorknob and, coolest of all, *real shingles on the roof!*

Beyond the shadow of a doubt, Daddy was the prince of my little life. He loved each of his seven children in huge-but-equal doses, and we knew for a fact that he'd move heaven and earth to please and protect us. I'm telling you the truth: The man loved me so much, he even pretended to eat my yucky, dripping mud pies. He once spilled an entire pie in his lap, and we both laughed until our stomachs hurt.)

Mama continued with her story, building steam like a quiet locomotive.

"The saleslady on the phone even asked for my name and I told her proudly, 'Mrs. James W. Clark,'—she even promised to hold it for me in the back until I could get there, which I thought was quite kind."

My mind painted the picture of Mother, legs crossed, sitting at the small telephone table in the little nook between the kitchen and the front hallway, patiently looking up the phone number for the store in our thick Yellow Pages, then dialing the number on our heavy-as-a-load-of-bricks black rotary telephone. I'm sure she smiled inside when the saleslady so graciously offered to put the hat on hold for her until she arrived. Mother always did appreciate good service. Imagining Mother smiling made me smile, too, if only by way of that magical mother-child osmosis.

I pushed, eager. "Then what happened, Ma? What happened when you got there?"

My heart was pounding as though I was hearing the story for the first time. That's how it was with Mother. Everything she touched was forever fresh. Startlingly alive. Crackling with color, energy, and truth.

"Well, honey, I cleared a path through that crowd of shopping women like Moses parting the Red Sea. I was moving through that store like there was no tomorrow. I was on a *mission*, baby. A hat-buying mission."

Silence from me. Breath-holding. I swear. I was pretty dramatic for a seven-year-old.

"Even as I made my way through all those pushy women and cackling hens, I kept praying that the saleslady had remembered to keep my hat on hold. I'd just finished making a navy blue A-line dress with a white-ribbon collar that would match it perfectly. In fact, I picked the fabric for my dress especially for this hat I was about to buy. I just *knew* they would look perfect together."

Mother was an expert seamstress, sewing many of our dresses, lined jumpers, and sometimes even our winter coats. She was darned proud of it, too. I wanted her to feel her own pride, so I made her describe the hat and dress again for me, so she could hear the words in her own ears.

"Oh, that dress fit my body like a glove, Beauty. I didn't even use a pattern for that one. I just went by sight, feel, and pure desire."

"And the hat, Ma. Describe the hat in the store."

"A sharp-looking little navy blue pillbox, dainty and as ladylike as could be. It was one fine hat, Beauty, let me tell you . . . But you know that already now, don't you?" she asked, smiling down into my face.

I had the distinct feeling, at that moment, that if I'd sat up and looked at her square in the face, I'd have seen her eyes glistening. Maybe with sad tears. Maybe with the immediacy and urgency of the memory she was describing, still

obviously fresh in her mind. At this point in the story, the
hairs at the nape of my neck always stood up at full attention. It was definitely the most compelling part of the plot,
but also the most painful and unpleasant. Even for my seven-
year-old heart.

The sound and smell of fat raindrops on hot asphalt
wafted into our living room, but neither of us made a move
to get up and close the living room window. Wet-earth
smells blew in. Another rumble of thunder, closer now, as
the sky prepared to crack open and pour. I snuggled in
closer to her and hung on tightly, her clingy, cloying papoose.
I could hear the sound of softly creaking floorboards upstairs
as my sister padded from one room to the next, continuing
to pull the bedroom windows closed against the rain.

"What happened when you got there, Ma? When you
asked Mrs. Crenshaw if you could try on the hat just once
before you bought it?"

After hearing the story so many times, I already knew the
saleslady's name—as well as what happened next. A slow
simmer began at the fringes of my soul, along with a downright thunderous rumble in the pit of my stomach—not the
place that rumbles when you're hungry, but when you're
angry.

Or worried.

Or scared.

A pause. Heavy, leaden silence. Mother gazed down at

me and tugged gently on one of my pigtails, all fuzzy from
the thick summer humidity.

"Mrs. Crenshaw just stood there staring at me like she'd
lost her ever-loving mind—as if she'd just seen a three-
headed Martian with polka-dot arms and two hundred little
legs do a backward somersault in the middle of the hat
department," Mother said, making a weak attempt at humor-
ous imagery to distract me from what was to come next.

But there would be no distractions. I was having none of
that. Mother continued, in her high-pitched, saleslady voice:

"'*You're* the lady who's been calling on the phone about the
pillbox?'" She was right-on with her imitations, my mother.

The air around us grew thicker. I blinked rapidly.

"What'd you say then, Ma? How'd you answer?"

"First, I looked her steady in her eyes. And then I answered
nice and slowly, just in case she didn't understand," Mother
said, the slightest tone of condescension splashing around in
the currents of her voice. I envisioned her standing there eye
to eye with Mrs. Crenshaw, slowly, carefully enunciating
every word in slow-motion dignity.

"'Yes, that would be me.'"

She was a riot, my mom; perfect in her elocution and
razor-sharp with her wit. *"That would be me."* Who even speaks
like that in normal conversations?

She continued recounting her conversation with Mrs.
Crenshaw.

"'You and I have spoken on the telephone several times about the hat—and you *are* Mrs. Crenshaw, correct?'" Mother asked.

I always thought it was slightly weird that Mother would have asked the saleslady her name since back then all salesladies were required to clearly display their employee badges on their lapels. This saleslady, I imagined, wore hers proudly and as big as day so that it would be hard to miss, perfectly pinned to the right lapel of her fancy-shmancy suit. But Mother never did anything without a reason. There was definitely a reason she'd asked the salesclerk to repeat her name.

"Well, Krissy," Mother continued, smiling sadly now while fingering another fuzzy, flyaway tendril of my hair, "you know your mother never did get that hat."

"Why, Ma? Tell me again why."

"Because Mrs. Crenshaw told me she hadn't realized when she'd spoken to me all those times on the phone that"—and here, a pursing of her lips so slight it was almost imperceptible—"the store management had suddenly changed their policy and they were no longer able to put merchandise on hold, especially hats."

We sat quietly together as the sky finally cracked wide open and the rain fell down in sheets.

"What happened when you asked if you could at least try the hat on?" I asked, my heart leaping and lurching forward inside my chest like the Little Engine That Could.

"She told me I couldn't *even try the hat on* . . . that if I tried it on, I'd have to buy it. And if I got home and decided I didn't like it, 'returning it was not an option.'"

Outside on our street, I could hear bicycle tires swishing along the rain-soaked pavement—either mucho-macho Curtis proving to everybody that he didn't care whether his bike rusted or not, or show-offy Sheila, who used to be my friend until the week before, when she'd called me a skinny-legged beanpole. (Sheila was my friend, but she'd become a little show-offy since she'd just gotten a brand-new banana bike. Jeez. I had a banana bike, too—but did anyone ever hear *me* constantly flapping my gums about how great I thought it was? No sirree. My parents taught me better than that. Bragging was forbidden, under any circumstances.)

Mother, wide awake now and more alert than ever, forged ahead with her story.

"'Well, I'd say that sounds mighty strange, wouldn't you agree, Mrs. Crenshaw? All of these sudden changes in store policy only just going into effect *the minute* I walk into the store and you see my face?'"

Mrs. Crenshaw, by then, must have been a real nervous Nellie. Mother imitated her again:

"'I cannot speak to whether or not you regard our store policies as "strange," ma'am,'" the old battle-ax said to my mother, "'but I would certainly hope you'd appreciate the fact that we can't just have *everybody* parading in here wanting to try on hats before they buy them, and begging for them to be put on hold. From a business standpoint, trying on the hats discourages the other women—prospective buyers, I might add—from trying on and purchasing the same merchandise afterward. It's simply a *hygienic* issue, ma'am, not a personal one. I'm sure you can appreciate that.'"

"'Well if I can't even try on the hat, Mrs. Crenshaw, then I certainly won't be purchasing it.'"

"'Whatever you choose,'" Mrs. Crenshaw retorted. "'Now good day to you.'"

Then she turned her back on my mother to help another customer.

She turned her back on my mother.

Hatred was a sentiment I did not know well, not at that young age, because we were taught not to familiarize ourselves with its demonic intensity. Mother and Daddy dedicated their lives to teaching us that hatred only destroys. But this much I knew: I didn't *like* Mrs. Crenshaw one bit. She sounded stupid. Dumb. Ignorant. Mean. Most of all, she'd denied Mother something that she'd wanted very badly, and she'd snatched at Mother's dignity, trying—unsuccessfully— to rip it all to shreds. Still, the devil in my heart won over the God in my soul, so I said it:

"I *hate* Mrs. Crenshaw and I hope she's dead now," I said flatly and without apology.

The minute I said that, Mother leaned way over in shock

and anger—rather painful and viselike for me, what with my head being in her lap and all.

"Kristin Kay Clark, don't you *ever* let me hear you say you hate anyone! You know better. We do not hate."

She was pretty angry at me for saying it, but I didn't care. I *did* hate Mrs. Crenshaw, and I did hope that she had died. I'd already visualized her as old as dirt even back then. Certainly she'd be dead all these years later. Of *something*, I hoped. Heart attack, maybe. Or a car accident. Or maybe by getting one of her fancy high-heel pumps caught in a sidewalk grate and being run over by a bus.

"I'm sorry, Ma. I didn't mean it." Or maybe slipping in the bathtub and hitting her face on the faucet, then bleeding to death in her own bathroom.

"I should hope you *would* be sorry, young lady," Mother said in a hot but not white-hot whisper. She was cooling down a little but she was still pretty mad. I prayed she wouldn't tell Daddy when he came home from work. He'd give me one of his disapproving sidelong glances and involuntarily squint his eyes.

I wondered, then, whether Mother had ever really shared the full story, in all its detail, with any of my other siblings. It wasn't spoken of in our home. Maybe, I thought, it existed as a shared secret between the two of us. I kind of hoped it was.

"Keep going with the story, Ma. Let's just forget I ever said the 'hate' part. It's just that that part of the story always makes me mad. They should have let you buy that hat. They didn't even let you *try it on!*"

I think I used the word *hate* on that afternoon because it was the most venomous, vicious word I could muster up from my somewhat limited vocabulary. But even in my own seven-year-old soul, I realized that actual *hate*—particularly toward an entire race of people—did not exist in my heart. In fact, most of my childhood schooldays—the first ten years, in fact—were spent in a predominately all-white world. Since kindergarten, I'd attended the Roeper School, a lushly landscaped private school located in Bloomfield Hills, an affluent suburb of Detroit. In the first few years of my attendance, there were only a few black students in the entire class, maybe three at the most. It was a sprawling campus that felt more like college than kindergarten. Roeper students were gentle, loving, and completely accepting of my brown skin. I had many close friends. Mother called it a "progressive" school, and she loved its unique, creative approach to educating the *whole* child—body, mind, and soul.

We called our teachers by their first names and often held classes outside. The campus sat on acres and acres of rolling hills, with swimming pools (two, I think) and sunny, private glens where you could cuddle up with your favorite book. I wrote my first poem in a tree house near what was then a wide, open field used for baseball games, raucous games of Red Rover, and fun-filled field-day activities. The main building of the campus was a refurbished mansion that sat majestically atop a high hill. We held our assemblies and ate our daily meals in what was once the great room of someone's home. The master bedrooms and suites were our comfortable classrooms; what had once been a wealthy family's attic had been charmingly, magically transformed into the art department. I'd never known anything like it.

Very beautifully, and with a sense of enlightened power and self-determination, my ten years at Roeper taught me how to nurture and maintain my spiritual and emotional equilibrium. The school seemed to have a spirit and a pulse. I was bountifully blessed to be within its protective embrace as I developed spiritually.

Not only the school but the *environment* within it proved a vital support system for me, a black child growing up in the turbulent '60s. Sure, spending every weekday and most early evenings completely surrounded by children of a different race sometimes felt a bit schizophrenic. There were many times when I felt like a high-wire artist trying to balance between two starkly different realities. I didn't realize until much later that my beloved Roeper School actually provided a strong, sturdy bridge between those two distinctly different worlds. Along with my close-knit family, Roeper filled my youthful heart with love and happiness. And throughout my childhood, the promise of inclusion and pure, human compassion were rare and wonderful life principles. My parents had been wise indeed to work so diligently to get me into that special school. My life had been—and still is, to this day—immeasurably strengthened because of the Roeper experience.

In fact, it was Mother and Daddy who sacrificed in order to ensure that my years at Roeper were fruitful and fascinating. The tuition was steep, and additional money was often required for extracurricular activities. And it was also the generosity of my older siblings—who contributed what they could toward my tuition, in addition to nurturing me emotionally and physically—that helped spur me forward.

As sad as my soul felt when it happened, my siblings eventually began to fly away from our safe little nest, launching out to begin their own exciting new lives. They were beginning to earn their own incomes, and they shared much of what they earned with Mother and Daddy, just because they knew it was the right thing to do and because their collective sense of familial responsibility was centered, generous, and selfless.

Their enduring commitment to "family first" and their unrelenting dedication to the notion—and practice—of one-helping-another enriched my life deeply. So even at age seven, they'd already showered me with such constant, unconditional love that I knew of nothing else. I grew up believing—*knowing*, with absolute clarity of mind—that to give and receive love, in its purest form, was effortless and all-encompassing, as were the principles of kindness, respect, and spiritual generosity. From the moment I was born and ever since, it has been my family who has imprinted these values deep into my heart. It is part of who I am.

Despite all that, though, I remained resentful and angry about what had happened to my mother when she'd tried to buy that precious church hat all those years ago, long, long before she'd even brought me into this world. Each time I listened to her church hat story, it made me want to stick out my tongue or look cross-eyed at the first person I saw.

But on that afternoon, all I wanted was for her to keep talking.

"What happened next?" I asked, though I already knew.

Stretching, catlike, she rose and turned toward the open window and closed it. Through the window screen, the rain sprayed a fine mist on her forearms. I thanked God for the mist. For her arms. For the raindrops that had finally found their way into our comfortable house and home. She was focused again, and answered my question quickly.

"Well, I turned around, walked right out of that store, crossed the street, and caught the bus back home. Out of the corner of my eye, I could see Mrs. Crenshaw already helping another customer. And guess what she was doing, Beauty?" she asked.

I knew the answer, but it was too painful to say aloud.

"She was helping that other woman try on *my* hat," Mother answered for me.

My heart told me that the woman who was trying on

Mother's hat had to have been white, even though Mother never specified. She didn't have to mention the color of the other customer's skin or the saleslady's bigoted behavior; not at that moment, anyway. It would have been rude and unseemly, which Mother was not.

A sudden crash of thunder made me jump. Kaboodle, no longer statue-like under the table, dashed like a furry bolt of lightning into the kitchen through the louvered living room door. The thunderclap seemed to shift the ions in the room, and the newly arranged energy helped steer us gently toward the happy, redemptive conclusion of the story.

"That very next Saturday, I went down to the fabric store. By the end of that day, I want you to know that I had myself a beautiful hat that I'd made with my own hands. You know the very hat, honey, because it's still sitting upstairs in that flowered hat box in the attic—right next to my Forever Box. I'm keeping it fresh, so that you can remember this story, and maybe even tell it to your own children one day, decades from now—long, long after I'm gone."

The very idea of Mother leaving me—whether it was to go to work, run an errand, or even just to answer the phone—was unsettling enough. The notion of her *dying* was, to me, simply unfathomable. (Heavens to Betsy! I didn't even like it when she took an afternoon *nap*, simply because it took her away from me for those precious few moments!) No sirree. I was having absolutely none of that "when-I'm-gone" nonsense. Not from Mother.

The other thing she'd said that unsettled my nerves was all that stuff about one day having children of my own. Those words caused an immediate and severe burning sensation deep in my chest, in that hard-to-reach place behind my rib cage and my spine. I wondered and worried, in my own little head, *Wait a ham-sandwich minute! What in the world was she talking about—having my own children one day?*

Absurd.

Hogwash.

Malarkey.

At seven going on eight, I didn't even want to spend one ounce of emotional energy trying to visualize myself with my own children, if only because I was still one myself. In fact, I didn't want to spend one ounce of energy focusing on anything else besides the softness of Mother's skin and how happy I was—at that precise moment—to be able to inhale her magical Mother smells.

໕

I REMEMBER the shooting pangs of pride I felt toward Mother on that stormy summer afternoon, not only for having faced the indignity of racial prejudice with such grace, but for pushing so powerfully through such a dark moment in order to "make it to the other side of bad"—to that place that was positive and solution-driven.

Mother had been mistreated, denied, and turned away, but that had not deterred her. If anything, it served to spur her forward, catapulting her toward her own creativity and resourcefulness. She'd crafted a solution within her own mind about reasonable alternatives—and the by-product was something more beautiful than even she could have imagined. That it happened to unfold from a simple, unfortunate church hat experience was fortuitous indeed. In one simple story, she'd taught me how to leapfrog over some of the ugliness in world around us.

The fact that she was asking me to keep her church hat so that I could one day share it with my own children was lost on me at that young age. Today, I recognize the rationale behind her request: She wanted me to show her hat to my children so that they, in turn, could absorb important life lessons about pride, resourcefulness, and self-respect.

Needless to say, today, Mother's hat sits perfectly preserved in its original hatbox. My prayer today is that my children will be wise enough to preserve both the hat *and* the story behind it, passing it along to successive generations so that it never ever dies. And if they, in turn, teach their own children the same lessons, this comforting, cyclical pattern will continue—and Mother's lessons about life and love will live on, quite literally, forever.

However, on that rainy summer afternoon, the only thing I needed was Mother. I knew nothing of cyclical patterns or life lessons or the preservation of principles. What I *did* know was that Mother was now fully awake and close, and I was content. I never wanted this moment in time to come to an end.

So what did I do? First, I completely dismissed her preposterous prediction that one day she'd be gone. I totally forced it out of my seven-year-old mind. Second, I reached up from my spot on the sofa and pulled her back down toward me, laying my little head in her warm, inviting lap.

Eventually, Mother and I both fell asleep to the rolling, rumbling sounds of that magical summer thunderstorm.

I'm certain that I dreamed about her church hat as we napped that afternoon.

How do I know?

Because it was the first time I think I ever smiled in my sleep.

～

TODAY, I know precisely what Mother's pillbox hat looks like because I keep it carefully stored in its original hatbox, painstakingly wrapped in layers and layers of tissue paper, bubble wrap, and clear cellophane. And anytime the spirit moves me, I can reach into my hatbox, hold the hat tenderly in my hands, and allow the memories of that magical afternoon with Mother to seep directly into my soul. Not only the hat—but the story behind it—help sustain Mother's legacy, and before I leave this earth I will pass it along to my own two children, who will pass it on to theirs.

No, Mother's hat cannot fit comfortably within the dim confines of my mahogany, cedar-lined Forever Box—but that's just fine with me. I know where it is when I need it—and, like Mother said that summer afternoon, it is, indeed, "one fine hat!"

What *does* fit comfortably into my box? The original copy of *Black Beauty*, the one Mother used to read to me regularly as a child. Many of the pages are dog-eared from use and yellowed with age, but the memories still burn brightly, as will Mother's sweet, sweet spirit.

A Forever Box can take many different forms, whether it's a hatbox, a hope chest, or even something as simple as a wicker basket. Creating a repository in which to house and hold the most pleasing and positive parts of our past is the most important element of memory-making.

It's also vital to keep in mind that the power of preservation lies not only in collecting tangible trinkets and beautiful baubles, but in the ability to pass down from one generation to the next the family values and principles that were once held so dear by our ancestors. It is possible for an entire belief system to remain intact, not just for days but for decades—into perpetuity, in fact—if we're purposeful about precisely how and what we want to preserve for our children and our children's children.

Principles and life lessons about kindness, compassion, faith, and friendship can all live forever if we work hard to pass them down with care and caution to those newly born and yet-to-be born. What a comfort it is to know that our vision and values can burn on as brightly as the North Star—but only for as long as we fan their flames.

And how long is that?

Forever.

If we do it right.

SCRATCH BISCUITS

--- ❧ ---

THE NEXT MORNING, it was still raining. I know this because I heard the *ffflliitt, ffflliitt* sound of bicycle tires swishing past our house. My bedroom window was open slightly, and a few fat raindrops made their way through the screen, landing on my windowsill then bouncing down onto the crown of my nose. The rider seemed to be circling continuously and directly below my window. I knew it was Sheila, a girl in my neighborhood who'd just gotten a brand-new banana bike—and she wanted everyone to know it, too! Show-off to the nth degree.

I decided to put her out of my mind and to put jealousy out of my heart—at least for the time being. I had something important planned for the morning, and nothing was going to get in my way. I rose and stretched, then lowered myself to my knees for my morning prayer. *Thank you, God, for letting me rise to see a bright new day. Please watch over me and my family throughout the day, and take care of the people who are sad or sick, like Mr. Grassley down the street, who has the gout in his left foot; and poor Miss Beulah, who fell clean through her back porch when she stepped on that piece of rotted wood. I love you, Lord. And I know that You love me. Please keep everybody safe and don't let Kaboodle get hit by a car since you already know how he loves trying to catch those sparrows that are always hopping near the curb.*

After washing up quickly in our upstairs bathroom, I heard Daddy's whistle. He was an excellent whistler, my father. I loved the way he'd wet his lips, quick like a snake, then let out his short, staccato-like chirp; Father Bird sending out the signal for his baby chicks to gather close around him.

From the sound of his whistle, I could tell he was standing at the bottom of the stairs, calling us all down to breakfast. That's kind of how Daddy communicated. By whistling. Or sidelong glances. Or maybe a slow smile that would make its way across his face when he was simply happy to be close to us. He was indeed a man of few words, yet he managed to get his point across more effectively than just about anybody I knew. Go figure.

Because there were so many of us—and because he used words so sparingly—Daddy devised his own unique way of communicating with us, and we all understood him instinctively and completely. His whistling was an excellent (and entertaining) way of getting our immediate and collective attention—whether we were at a picnic in the park or scattered in different rooms throughout our house.

I spent long summer nights with Cookie, who lived right next door. We'd whisper and giggle and sometimes play tag with our father's flashlights (as long as they didn't notice, because both men were kind of fussy about their flashlights. They'd get all salty about our running the batteries down, so we didn't play flashlight tag all that often. It just wasn't worth it, especially since there were so many other fun things for the two of us to get into on warm summer nights.).

Cookie's father, too, had his own unique whistle, a beckoning call for his youngest daughter to drop everything and come a-running. When Mr. Pounds, a tall, elegant man who loved his wife and three daughters with that same father-passion as Daddy, came out onto his porch and let out his smooth-sounding warble, we both knew it was time to end our evening. We'd hug each other good-bye, then make mad dashes toward the safety of our homes, each pulled like little moths toward the brightened porch lights that beckoned us back to our families.

On this particular gray and stormy morning, breakfast was warm and waiting (the whistle told us as much), so we all trampled downstairs and grabbed our seats at the kitchen table. Time for more prayer. Before each and every meal, we always said the Blessing of the Food in unison—all nine of us. *Gracious Father, we truly thank You for the food we're about to receive, for the nourishment of our bodies, in Christ's sake. Amen.*

I was always so *excited* to be sitting at the kitchen table with my parents and siblings, my short legs dangling and swinging happily under a table crowded with sixteen other knees, legs, and feet. I also think I might have been the praying-est seven-year-old on the block; two prayers within the first fifteen minutes of the day! Praying seemed to settle down my small spirit. And whenever I spoke to God, I was certain that He was listening closely (even though I always imagined Him performing about thirty million other tasks at the same time, like making sure all the airplanes in the sky didn't go crashing into one another and making sure the sun wasn't shining in Nairobi and Nantucket at the same time. He had quite a lot to do—this much I knew for sure—but I also knew that he *always* had time to listen to my prayers).

When it came to praying, I'd also devised this secret trick, which I haven't shared with anyone else until now: If you squeeze your eyes shut real tight while you pray, I'm pretty sure God can hear you better. And for really important prayers, squeeze your eyes shut as tightly as you can, cross your fingers on both hands and scrunch up the toes on your left foot all at the same time. (Toe-scrunching is pretty hard, especially when you're wearing sneakers or rubber

rain boots, but trust me, it can be done in emergencies.)
Daddy probably wouldn't have liked it, and I could already
hear his quiet but stern disapproval: "You don't need to perform any tricks or engage in any high jinks to communicate
with the Lord, Buttercup. He's always with us—leading us,
guiding us—and He always hears our prayers. Quiet, private prayer, without a lot of banging around, is the best way
to still your soul—and even seven-year-old girls with fuzzy
pigtails and pretty smiles need stillness and peace in their
lives. So talk to Him more often, Buttercup . . . And don't let
me catch you crossing your fingers or scrunching your toes
while you're doing it!"

Yes, indeed. My father was a man's man; a doting daddy
with many hidden talents. Besides whistling, he was also an
excellent fisherman. Preparing for a fishing excursion with
Daddy was just about as much fun as the excursion itself. The
night before, we'd water our front lawn for about fifty thousand hours (I often worried that we'd flood the house), then
we'd wait. Later that same night, when everyone else was
sleeping, and the water had had a chance to soak into the
soil real good, we'd grab two flashlights and our Maxwell
House coffee tin, which was already filled with dark, rich
soil. Stooped at the waist, trying like all get-out to spy a
bloodworm or two rising to the surface of the grass, my
father and I would speak in whispered tones. I always yelped
with excitement whenever I spied one of the squiggly things.

"Quiet, Buttercup! You'll scare them back into the ground!"
Daddy would say, a half-smile passing over his shadowed sil-
houette. With great care and concentration, I'd squat down
and pull the heartiest worms ever so gently from their soil.
There was a certain way you had to catch those slippery guys,
too—and you had to be quick as lightning. Surprisingly, they
could squirm back into the warm, wet earth real fast, and
many times they'd wiggle away before I could get a good
enough grip to pull them from the earth. Daddy taught me to
plunge my fingers into the soil quickly, with a sudden thrust,
then pull the worm out as gently as possible. Sure, one reason
he wanted us to be gentle with those worms was because they
could tear in half if we pulled too hard. (I know. Gross.) But
the most important reason, I still believe to this day, was
because he simply didn't want those worms to suffer. That's
the way Daddy was—as gentle as a cool breeze and as kind as
a grandmother or maybe even a nun.

After we collected about thirty of the squirming things, we
covered the top of the coffee tin with aluminum foil. Daddy
would let me use the sharp knife to poke holes in the foil so
the worms could breathe a little (it was the only time I was
allowed to handle kitchen knives, so for me, it felt adventurous and daring). Then we'd get upstairs and fall fast asleep.

Only minutes after my head hit the pillow (or so it seemed),
Daddy was kneeling beside me, gently shaking me awake.
"Wake up, Buttercup!" he'd say in an excited whisper. "It's time

to shake a leg! If we don't move now, all the fish will swim to the other side of the river and all we'll catch is tin cans and old rubber boots!" A warning such as this always made me leap right up and shimmy straight out of my warm bed into the peaceful (and somewhat frightening) predawn morning.

It was always dark outside when we began our fishing expeditions. Those quiet morning moments with Daddy, moving around silently in the kitchen, trying to pack our cheese sandwiches with only the night-light to guide us, were some of the most precious in my life. I loved the feel of our spacious, creaking house during those magical moments as the sky turned from midnight black to a deep, cobalt blue. It somehow felt like our house was sleeping (or at least breathing) all by itself.

Moving carefully down the darkened steps into the basement, we'd continue our father-daughter, getting-ready-to-go-fishing routine. Just at the bottom of the stairs, Daddy would pick me up so that I could reach the string that hung from the ceiling. One quick tug on that string—*click*—and soft, yellow light immediately illuminated everything around us. (Thank goodness. Our basement was scary, and I was never a huge fan of the dark. I know, I know, I was Scared Susie. Kind of a wimp. But of this I was fairly certain: There were mean little snaggle-toothed monsters that lived under our basement stairs, and they only came out when Daddy and I were moving around down there in the dark.)

We knew just what to do, my father and I, and usually we did it in complete silence. In the basement, it was my job to pull out the fishing rods and position them carefully at the bottom of the stairs. Daddy carried up the rods and his heavy, metal tackle box. My job was to bring up the Maxwell House can of worms and our woven fishing basket. (I always started to feel a little sad for those unsuspecting worms, though. They were so comfortable and happy in their rich, dark soil; so completely unsuspecting of the terrible fate that was soon to befall them . . . It was bad enough to get skewered with a hook—but to get gobbled up by a hungry perch, too? Just plain cruel. I wasn't sure God liked such cruelty. But I figured if Daddy didn't think it was cruel, then it couldn't be cruel; so I'd trip happily up the steps behind him, excited as all get-out.)

Loading the station wagon usually required two trips. It was my responsibility to bring along the bagged lunches: usually two cheese sandwiches, a couple of apples, a few extra slices of bread, and a big bag of Cracker Jack (of course Daddy always let me keep the prize inside). The extra bread, Daddy always said, was "for the fish, just in case they're in the mood to eat it."

The very last task I always performed before we headed out was to check the tackle box for an extremely important item: In one of the small compartments, Daddy always kept an old, tiny copper bell, which he'd hang at the very tip of my pole as soon as we got to the pier. I loved that old bell. Whenever we were fishing and I'd hear its soft tinkle, I'd just about faint from excitement—because it meant a fish was on the other end of my line! An actual *fish*—with gills and fins and a tail that was still flopping around, even after we'd reeled him in! (Immediately after unhooking the fish from our line, we'd drop it into our reed basket and submerge the basket in water so that the poor thing wouldn't suffocate.) Yes, indeed, catching a fish with Daddy was more adventurous than climbing to the top of Mount Everest. More exhilarating than stepping off the edge of the world. Even more fun than riding the Tilt-a-Whirl and the Zipper at the state fair.

Once we set off down the road, we'd usually drive to Belle Isle because they had the best piers. Many times we'd even go to Canada, since it was just across the river. (What other seven-year-old could boast that she'd fished with her father in two different countries within the short span of only one summer?)

Whenever I caught a fish, Daddy made it seem like I was the only person on the face of the earth, and like I had just performed a modern-day miracle. After I reeled it in (he'd always let me reel in my own catch), he'd inspect the fish really closely, then give me this serious-but-silly-looking salute. Then he'd gently hook his strong arms under my armpits and twirl me around and around in happy, happy circles.

We could be at the pier at Belle Isle, or the lake at Palmer Park or even on the other side of the bridge in Canada, and he'd *still* twirl me around and around. Shoot, there could be a hundred other people around. No matter. Daddy and I danced our Just-Caught-a-Fish dance no matter where we were or who else was watching. I could not have been more loved.

Although Daddy has long since left this earth, the tiny copper bell he gave me an entire lifetime ago remains with me. It's tucked away in a corner of my Forever Box, and when you shake it gently, it still tinkles. And every time I look at it today—every time I shake it gently to hear its soft tinkle—I think of Daddy. Now, on a regular basis, I share with my two children those famous fishing stories of long ago. Stories about worm hunts and fishing poles. Of copper bells and Cracker Jack. Of moving around in those quiet, predawn hours and the Maxwell House coffee tin that lasted throughout my entire childhood.

I consider it a heavenly privilege and a Divine honor that God allowed the passage of time to overlap onto itself so that my own children, when they were very small, had the opportunity to go fishing with my father, too. And fish they did. I only wish I could have witnessed it more clearly the first time Daddy took them out, but my vision was blurred by the tears of happiness that were stinging my eyes. There it was, right before me: a real-life vision of not only two but *three* generations of fishing happiness. (And yes, Daddy would take my kids to a spot on Belle Isle that was very near the same spot we'd enjoyed a lifetime earlier.)

Both the three-generational fishing memories *and* my precious copper bell will exist long after I leave this place. And what will also exist, because I have shared these fishing stories with my children, are the memories of those early morning excursions and how brave I felt bustling around so busily in those dark, predawn hours, doing the Just-Caught-a-Fish dance with my father.

COURTESY OF THE AUTHOR

And although this obviously cannot fit into my Forever Box simply because it's not an actual bauble or trinket, here's something else that can be passed along from one generation to the next, which Daddy helped instill in my spirit: the power of unconditional love. It doesn't have to be a loud, clanging love; it can be completely silent. Daddy taught me that feeling love is important, of course—but *showing* it is equally vital, and such a demonstration need not always be dripping with syrupy words and sentimental sayings. Such huge, gulping doses of love can involve slippery worms, soggy cheese sandwiches, and even sharp-toothed hairy monsters that live under the basement stairs.

ॐ

AFTER breakfast that morning, we all fell into the familiar, collective rhythm of cleaning up our bright yellow kitchen. Each person had a task. Usually (but not always), I'd wipe the table clean and dry the plates, while another sibling returned the forks and knives to the silverware drawer beside the stove. (I'd always yearned for the task of wiping down our white enamel teapot, which always sat on the left rear burner of the stove, but Mother wouldn't allow it until I was taller.)

But on *this* morning, I snuck away from my kitchen chores early because I needed to check on something important. I opened our screen door and stepped out onto the front porch. The rain fell hard and heavy, and one upward glance revealed a low-hanging sky of gray gossamer. Fat, blood-red worms wiggled this way and that on the asphalt, happy to be out from underneath the dark earth. But the worms weren't what I was focusing on at that moment. I had a mission to accomplish.

Peering across the street, I saw exactly what I was looking for. Even through the rain, I could see her: my friend Mrs. Luella Rae Simpson, sitting on her front porch. Her lowered head told me she was either praying, reading her Bible, or was fast asleep. Whatever the case, I knew that her mere presence on the porch was a signal to me, an unspoken invitation to let me know that it was fine for me to come over for a visit.

I tried to run between the raindrops to avoid getting thoroughly soaked as I dashed across to her house. Even as I ran, I whispered quick, shooting prayers for the unsuspecting worms in the street because, sure as shooting, they were about to get squashed by the tires of passing cars. *Just wait till Mr. Fisher swings his shiny blue Rambler into his driveway when his shift lets off at Ford. Squish! Splat! Keep these little worms safe, Lord. Tell them to go back down into the grass before it's too late.* Those poor smashed worms wouldn't even be suitable bait for our fishing days.

The moment she saw me running toward her, ol' Mrs. Simpson leaned forward in her rocking chair and started hollering.

"Look both ways before you cross that street, missy!" she yelled loudly. I swear, the woman was always screaming. And even as I ran, I could just *feel* the passionate prayers she was shooting in my direction, asking God to get me safely to the other side of the street. I could tell—by the sheer decibel level of her voice—that she was genuinely concerned about the possibility of my getting flattened by a passing car, just like Mr. Fisher was about to flatten all those worms.

I was running like the wind, raindrops pelting my hair, hands and arms. But even in the corner of my mind, I could feel myself worrying about whether nosy Sheila was peeking out of her window, spying on me. Of course, in my effort to avoid as many raindrops as possible, I ran zigzag all the way there, so it took me a little more time than usual to get to Mrs. Simpson's house.

As much as I loved my friend, I sure wished she'd quiet down. And although I hated to admit it, even as I was hoofing it across the street, I could feel the hot flames of embarrassment beginning to burn my brown cheeks. *Why'd she absolutely insist on doing all that hootin' and hollering? What if she fell out of her rocker or something like that?* Show-off Sheila would never have let me hear the end of it. I imagined the sound of Sheila's voice; a tense, teasing whisper directly into my ear: "Why are you best friends with a hundred-year-old woman anyway?" I could hear her asking me with disdain.

Just as quickly, God came in close and slapped all that embarrassment right off my slender shoulders. He reminded me that Mrs. Simpson was my *friend*—and a good one, too. She was as excited to see me as I was to see her. We were bosom buddies.

But her barking continued, sounding a little like a seal.

"Watch out! I *know* you see that car coming down from Oakland Street, don't you?" she yelled again, leaning even farther out of her rocker now. I was beginning to think that all the excitement with the rainstorm and the approaching car and my upcoming visit might have been too much for her. It might give her a heart attack or something. But Luella Rae Simpson was as strong as an ox; always was, from what I could remember. When her husband was alive (I don't remember him well; I was very young when he died), I watched her one day from our hallway window as she lifted up the back of their car while he scrambled underneath to rattle around near the rear axle, fiddling around with something that required a wrench. Or at least I *think* she lifted that car up by herself. (If there was a jack involved, I definitely didn't see it.) Plus, when her husband scrambled out from underneath the car, she let the car down nice and easy-like, snapped at her house dress with her dish rag, then calmly walked back inside to finish boiling her collards. No joke. When I tell you, you'd better believe it: She was strong as an ox. There would be no heart attacks today.

"Just wait till that car passes, baby, then come on across!" she continued in her loud, flat voice.

"Did you hear me, girl? I'm telling you to *wait* a ham-sandwich minute!"

Now she was gesturing wildly, making all kinds of warning signs with her hands. I did listen. And I did see the car, too. It was a full block away. I could have easily made it—even with my strategic, zigzag pattern—but, out of deference to Mrs. Simpson, I stopped at the curb and waited for the car to pass. It was an candy-apple-red T-Bird going much too fast, and as it passed by, dirty rainwater splashed all over me, all the way up to my neck. Jumping jackrabbits! Mother had just washed my cotton jumper that morning.

Mrs. Simpson saw the whole thing.

"Shouldna' been standing so close to the curb, missy!" she chided as soon as I'd climbed safely up the front stairs of her porch. "You might not have gotten your little narrow backside splashed from head to toe if you hadn't been standing so close to the street. Didn't you *hear* me hollering at you to wait?" she asked through a gentle smile, smacking her gums, which told me she didn't have her teeth in. Still, bless her heart, she had her handy dish towel ready the moment I arrived. For some strange reason she kept that dish towel with her everywhere she went, even if she was moving from the living room to the kitchen—but *this* time it actually came in handy. She reached in close to dry my rain-sprayed face in gentle plucks and pats, smacking softly and shaking her head in mock disgust.

"Chil', you're soaked to the bone," she muttered, leaning even farther forward to wipe down my skinny arms and large potato-shaped knees. *Don't let her topple over, God. Let her keep her balance and pleasepleaseplease protect her from falling out of her rocking chair.*

"Plus, you just keep growing like a weed!"

I could tell she was genuinely thrilled to see me. Really, truly happy.

She kept on: "You were just over here a few days ago, and I do declare you look a good half-inch taller since then. I should toss you out back with the rest of the beautiful weeds in my garden," she said, pulling me in close for a hug.

Mrs. Simpson smelled like mothballs, boiled chicken, and Vicks VapoRub. Not a bad or unpleasant kind of smell, just an *old-people's* smell, like when you sniff the inside of an overcrowded closet or maybe when you crawl up into your attic on a hot summer day. She also kind of cackled when she laughed, and she walked a little stooped over, because of her age and all.

She was pretty old, all right—and I really, truly loved the fact that she was so old! Why? Because she had loads of rich and wonderful real-life stories to share with me every time I visited, which is precisely why I spent time with her just about every other day (especially in the summers when school was out). I think I remember her telling me (but I can't confirm with 182 percent accuracy, since it happened so long go) that her parents had been sharecroppers, and her great-grandparents had been slaves. It was like being best friends with a walking, talking history book, except with a soft lap, a tender touch, and a loving heart. Yes, indeed. The two of us would spend hours rocking together on her front porch in the searing summer heat or retreating, finally, into the dimly lit rooms of her home (which somehow always remained cool, even though she didn't have air-conditioning).

A comfortable moment of silence stood between us. Finally, she spoke.

"You say your prayers this morning?" she asked matter-of-factly, studying my face carefully for an honest answer.

"In a way," I answered as honestly as I could. After all, I reasoned with myself, I *had* said my morning prayer as soon as I'd awakened, but it was shorter than usual, so I wasn't sure if it still counted. Plus, I'd prayed for the worms in the street, *and* we'd all said the blessing before breakfast, but I still didn't know if these were fervent and passionate enough for Mrs. Simpson's standards. Mrs. Simpson was one powerfully praying woman, by golly.

"Either you did or you didn't," she answered crisply, but without rancor or sarcasm.

"Well, then, yes, ma'am, I talked to God on my way over

here," I replied halfheartedly, relieved that I hadn't had to lie. It was true, I *had* talked to Him—briefly. Never mind that my prayer to Him had been about the bloodworms, or that my morning prayer had lasted only a few brief seconds. Something deep within me assured me, right then and there, as I was standing on her porch, that God doesn't discriminate or pass judgment on which prayer is more important than another. He listens to them all. Of *that*, I was sure, even if—but not just because—I scrunch up my toes.

"Always make time to pray, baby, no matter how busy you are. Jesus gave His entire life for us. The least we can do is give a moment of our own back to Him."

As usual, she was correct.

I made a mental note to put prayer in the center of my life—or try to, anyway. Mother and Daddy always seemed to keep God close around them, and I knew I had a responsibility to communicate with Him on a pure and fundamental level. Even though I was only seven, I knew that everything was in God's hands, and that His hands were guiding everything.

The only problem was that I didn't always have the *time* to pray. My playhouse out back always beckoned. There were fireflies to be caught in the dark of night. There was the magnetic pull of Mother's lilting voice that distracted me from my prayer time as well, especially on the nights when we'd sit together reading *Black Beauty*. Then there was the ice-cream man in his slow-moving truck, the Pied Piper of our entire neighborhood who made every child in a five-block radius drop whatever they were doing to come a-running.

Of all the things that could have—and did—distract me from whatever I was doing (even *praying*—sorry, God), I think the ice-cream man was the most powerful. The far-off, melodic tinkling sound of his truck was enough to make *any* child rise up from their knees mid-prayer. Mrs. Simpson would have been so, so disappointed. No doubt, the ice-cream man had more power and pull in our neighborhood than Martin Luther King Jr. himself. (No disrespect meant to Dr. King, but it's true. Or at least put it this way: If any child on my block saw two people walking down the street toward them, one being Martin Luther King Jr. and the other being the ice-cream man, I'm pretty sure they'd run like the wind toward the ice-cream man, nickels and pennies in hand. It's just how the kids in my neighborhood were.)

Our *parents*, however, were an entirely different story. Inside just about every neat, well-kept home on our block were what I called the FEOs—the Four Essential Objects. The first: a framed color photograph of Martin Luther King Jr. The second: an aged and yellowed palm frond from the most recent Palm Sunday service (usually tucked or taped behind the King photo), a family Bible, and the latest issue of *Ebony* magazine displayed on the living room table. I saw these as important indicators of the abiding faith and pride that existed within our close community. (To this day, I still have my grandmother's palm frond from a Palm Sunday service she attended probably long before I was even born.)

So no, our parents weren't anywhere near as excited about the ice-cream man as us kids.

But in our eyes, the ice-cream man was *magic*.

The very sound of that scratchy, repetitive little melody coming out of the speaker on top of his truck would stop kids in their tracks. If you were praying, you stopped (but not before promising God that you'd be back in five minutes). If you were in the middle of an argument with your best friend, you'd freeze first (to make sure that what you were hearing was, indeed, the sound of his truck), then you'd go a-running, promising to pick up the argument where you left off as soon as you finished your Nutty Buddy. Shoot, even if you were in the bathroom, for goodness' sake, you'd finish up at breakneck speed!

Kids scrambled wildly to get to their parents for spare change, hopping up and down like little jumping beans and crying, "Hurry *up*, Daddy! Find that quarter! The truck is driving away! He's *leaving*! Come *on*!" Then finally, the mad dash to catch the truck, because oftentimes he *had* turned the corner, to everyone's disbelief and disappointment. (And I know personally that there's *nothing worse* than missing the ice-cream man—whether it was because you were a dime or a nickel short, or because your prehistoric parents were embarrassingly slow at pulling their wallets out of their pockets, there's not really too much else that could be worse in a child's life.)

As if reading my mind, Mrs. Simpson continued:

"A long time ago, a saint of a man named Francis de Sales instructed people to commune with the Lord, no matter how busy they were," she said. "In fact, and let me see if I can remember this right"—she muttered almost to herself, pulling absently at the fraying hem of her housedress—"he said something like, 'We should all pray for at least fifteen minutes a day.'"

She sat still for a minute in heavy concentration, then continued, as if remembering the punch line to a joke. "'*Except* if we're too busy . . . then, we should pray for *thirty* minutes!'"

She really tickled herself with that one, laughing and wheezing and laughing some more at St. Francis's urgent plea for all of us to make time to pray more, no matter what else is on our busy agendas.

A sudden loud crack of thunder sent me straight into Mrs. Simpson's ample lap. I landed right on top of her Bible, hoping at that very moment that I hadn't committed some blasphemous sin by ripping the pages, which were as delicate as the skin of an onion—definitely not designed to withstand the sudden weight of a seven-year-old girl (even a skinny-legged beanpole like me). But she received me graciously, encircling me with both arms. As she hugged me, she let out another loud, whooping laugh (that cackle again), and she leaned over to place her heavy bible (the King James large-print version) on the floor so she could kiss me on top of my head.

"Think you can still fit that growing body of yours into my lap?" she asked with humor humming in her heart. All I knew was that I was content where I was—in her lap—even though her wrinkled skin (unlike Mother's) smelled slightly of mentholatum and old-people medicine. We sat together on her front porch rocking silently, happy to be together. Even as we rocked, though, I kept a keen eye out for Sheila, who'd never let me hear the end of it if she saw me being a big baby for sitting on the lap of a hundred-and-fifty-year-old lady.

After a few minutes, Mrs. Simpson stood up and settled me in the rocking chair while she shuffled back inside her house. The rain was still coming down in sure, steady sheets. From across the street, I watched our house. One of my siblings—I couldn't tell precisely which one because her face was obscured behind the screen—opened our front door to let Kaboodle out onto the porch. Our cat crouched at the edge of the top step, wary and reluctant to be outside, so close to the rain. I smiled when, only a moment later, a thin, golden female arm opened the door again, and Kaboodle dashed back into the warm safety of our house.

Minutes passed.

What in the Sam Hill was Mrs. Simpson *doing* inside her house for such a long time? Why would she leave me outside all by myself when we were supposed to be enjoying each other's company? Should I go check on her, just in case she'd tripped on the throw rug in her hallway or had a heart attack in the bathroom or gotten electrocuted by a faulty wire in her kitchen? A moment later, all of these questions were answered as the mouthwatering aroma of her homemade scratch biscuits came wafting through an open window. My heart danced a happy jig, and my little soul sent up a prayer of gratitude.

What touched me most deeply, though, was something far beyond her merely preparing those delicious biscuits. It tugged at my little heart to know that this sweet, Bible-reading, bent-over woman had actually taken the time to prepare for my arrival, all so that I could have a special treat. Her famous scratch biscuits aren't easy to make, either; there's the dough that needs to be prepared, then refrigerated for a time, followed by the time-consuming task of kneading the darned stuff. To say nothing of pulling out the wooden rolling pin and spreading that dough flat-as-a-pancake on the counter, then using a mason jar to cut out the circular shapes that transform the dough into beautiful round biscuits. You better know it, making scratch biscuits is more than a notion, and I felt honored that she'd gone to such trouble. I visualized her arthritic hands kneading the dough, and I really hoped it hadn't caused her any pain. I imagined her moving around in her kitchen, slowly pulling out eggs from her refrigerator, large enamel bowls from her cupboards, and then rooting through her pantry for the shortening. She'd made a huge effort on that rainy afternoon, and it certainly touched me deeply.

So I continued sitting there on the porch, pulling in the smell of Mrs. Simpson's baking, smiling like a Cheshire cat the whole time, my skinny legs dangling happily from her white wicker rocker. *Lord knows you should have lotioned those legs before you ran out of this house*, I heard Mother whispering to my imagination. *Not even a two-hundred-year-old woman, sweet as she is, wants to look at a pair of rusty, ashy knees, much less on a dreary day like this, Beauty! Pay more attention to your appearance!*

In that moment, I also began to worry a little that my body weight was probably becoming too much for Mrs. Simpson during our regular visits. Sure, she was miraculously robust and strong as an ox, but she was still as old as Methuselah. I decided I'd better sit in my own porch chair the next time I came over to visit. Goodness! The woman had about five chairs on her front porch! Why did I always insist on sitting in her *lap*? The last thing I wanted to do was harm her. She baked scratch biscuits and crocheted beautiful table doilies. She read to me from her Bible. She cared deeply about whether or not I'd be squished by a car as I crossed the street. She was one of my best friends.

Finally, I got up and walked into her house. I found her in the kitchen, leaning almost into the oven, checking on her biscuits. Because she was so old, I worried about her something terrible. As soon as she saw me, she straightened up to a standing position and nodded toward the kitchen table—which meant she wanted us to sit down and talk.

Uh-oh. Her head nodding worried me a little. *Was I in trouble?*

We sat together for a spell in comfortable but complete silence. I tried to look at her out of the corner of my eye to see if she'd fallen asleep (old people always seem to fall asleep in the middle of their sentences or while they're reading the Bible), but I was a little startled to see that she was staring directly at me, as alert as if she'd just had five or six cups of Maxwell House coffee. I cleared my throat. We listened to the wall clock tick-tocking away. Finally, I turned to watch her watching me. Her face looked thoughtful, maybe even a little worried. *Something's up*, I thought to myself. *She's got something on her mind.*

Sure enough, she started in:

"Just because you're in summer recess doesn't mean you stop studying your lessons, you know," she said, finally getting around to the point. It was too sweet. She was worried about her little friend, concerned that my brain would get rusty and slow-moving if I slacked on my summer homework.

"You been studying your lessons?"

Goodness me. Here it comes: The old "you-better-be-doing-your-homework" lecture. Jeez.

"Yes, ma'am," I lied handily and instinctively. Here I go again, on my way straight to hell for lying to Mother yesterday and Mrs. Simpson today. And more likely than not, Mrs. Simpson will leave this earth before I will because she's about a thousand years old, and I'm only seven. Drat it all! I won't even get to meet her in heaven, 'cause I will surely be in hell for lying.

But that didn't make me want her biscuits any less.

I knew for a fact that she couldn't eat her own scratch biscuits anymore. Although I'm not certain, I think I remember overhearing Mother talking quietly with my sisters one day, in hushed, worried tones, about Mrs. Simpson's "high blood pressure" and her "sugar dia-blee-teez." How was a seven-year-old to recognize the word *diabetes*? Somehow, these medical terms translated into the fact that poor Mrs. Simpson couldn't even enjoy her own baking! (Selfish to say, but I found myself smiling a little at this thought, because it meant *more for me!*)

"We'll get back to the subject of your lessons later," she said, still eyeing me suspiciously as though she just *knew* I hadn't cracked open my black-and-white marble notebook since school had let out a few weeks earlier. (Her instincts were right. I hadn't.) Despite myself, I was becoming a little impatient for those biscuits to be done. *How much longer? They're not burning, are they? You didn't forget about them, did you? Are you sure you even remembered to turn the oven on?*

She'd spooned some boiled cabbage from a pan on the stove into a large pink bowl, and she said a quick blessing before she began to eat. (She knew I had absolutely *zero* interest in cabbage—and that my sole reason for living was to scarf down her delicious biscuits the second they came out of the oven.) We continued sitting at the table together in comfortable silence—she gumming at that crazy cabbage, me sitting pensively, waiting for those darned biscuits to finish baking.

After about five or six minutes, I felt as if I *had* to get something off my chest: this ongoing, delicate matter of my being called a skinny-legged, potato-kneed beanpole, which hurt my feelings immensely. (I swear, my self-esteem swayed back and forth with as much regularity as the pendulum of my Aunt Lilly's grandfather clock.) I couldn't resist telling Mrs. Simpson—right there as we sat at her red-speckled kitchen table with shiny chrome legs and matching red vinyl chairs—about this nasty old name. I mean, really. A *skinny-legged beanpole*? Come on . . . and were my knees really, truly shaped like potatoes? I launched in, telling her exactly how I felt and explaining how much it had hurt my feelings.

Mrs. Simpson kept gumming away at her cabbage, though, not saying a word, but I could tell she was listening carefully as I blew off steam. She just kept chewing and looking at some invisible spot on her table and chewing some more. Shoving it in. I kind of wished she'd put in her teeth. Mother would have died a thousand deaths before sitting at anybody's table gumming away at food, much less without a tooth in her mouth. But Mrs. Simpson wasn't Mother. She was my friend. My toothless, cabbage-eating, biscuit-baking friend. And I loved her more than life itself.

Finally, she spoke.

"Let me get this straight. If someone calls you a three-legged horny toad, you just all of a sudden *become* a three-legged horny toad? Is that what I'm hearing from you, chil'?"

No sympathy from *her*, by golly. Not one bit. Not even an ounce.

She finally stopped chewing, though, and was studying me carefully. In the next second, she reached over to pull my chair closer to hers. I swear she was strong as an ox, that woman. She leaned in close to my face, the flat palms of both of her hands on either side of my cheeks. We were eye to eye. Even though her breath smelled kind of cabbagey, I listened attentively as she spoke.

"Your parents raised you to know that you are deeply loved by everyone around you—by both of them, of course, by your siblings, by your good friends, and—most important—by the sweet Lord Jesus Himself. You're a little brown queen, honey—and don't you ever let anybody tell you different. You understand?"

I nodded, feeling better already. Even my knees felt like they were shrinking down to their regular size, from oversized Idaho russet potatoes to, say, two medium-sized doorknobs. *Why did I allow self-doubt to cloud my thinking and knock me so off-center?*

Mrs. Simpson continued, newly fortified by my head nodding. "And you've got to learn that anybody who calls another person a mean name doesn't think very highly of herself, so what you've got to do is pray for them, honey. Be kind to her."

I gazed down at my feet, trying to make sense of Mrs. Simpson's instructions to be nice to everybody. I mean, I'd heard of turning the other cheek and all, but this was ridiculous. *Pray* for the person who'd likened my knees to a food that grows underneath the *dirt* and say nice things to the very person who may as well have called me a scatterbrained scarecrow? Come *on*.

But Mrs. Simpson meant business.

"It's unhealthy to let negative thinking and mean words float around in the universe. By fretting about those words, you're giving them way too much power. They're like little mean-spirited needles . . . trying to prick little holes into this beautiful balloon of ours that is God's loving universe."

I stopped breathing momentarily, disappointed. I wasn't quite sure what she meant about the universe and the pricked balloon and all, but I did understand the part about having to be kind, no matter what. I tried to replay Mrs. Simpson's words in my head.

Mrs. Simpson sat up straighter. The spirit of divine goodness and grace was moving in around her, fast and furious. I could feel it. "Always, always pray for those who hurt you, baby, no matter how hard it is," she said simply. "Be kind to her, not mean. Patient, not bitter."

She was on a spiritual roll now, and going to town on that cabbage: "I've always believed that kind deeds are like little prayers. And Lord knows we don't have enough of either in this world we live in today—kind deeds *or* little prayers." *Kind deeds are like little prayers.* I made a mental note to remember that phrase for when I got older. I liked the way it sounded. And then, as if in afterthought, she added: "And since when did you let somebody's name-calling get you all riled up and feeling poorly about yourself?" she asked, getting loud now, just like she had on the porch.

I didn't have an answer.

Then, with a saucy smile and a brightness of eye, she added, "And as fast as you're putting on weight, a 'beanpole' isn't what she should have called you at all. Maybe 'pudge' or a 'piglet,' but definitely not a beanpole. You're growing way too fast for that. Sounds to me like she might need glasses, 'cause she sure isn't seeing straight if she thinks you look like a beanpole. A *beanpole*? Ha!"

Mrs. Simpson was trying to be funny for my sake. She wanted to comfort her friend, to reassure her biscuit-eating buddy. It was so sweet I could have cried right then and there. I had an advocate. A protector. A best friend who boiled chicken and held my hand. I resisted the urge to ask her how she thought those biscuits were coming along; I was still a little worried she'd forgotten about them. And I knew Mrs. Simpson well enough to know that once she got started on subjects like the Lord or making the universe around us a healthier, happier place to live, there was really no stopping her.

I tried mightily to come up with a diversionary tactic. I mean, I love the Lord, too, and I believe in universal peace as much as the next person—but I thought I smelled the biscuits burning. I considered walking over to the sink to get a glass of water and then, by sheer coincidence and just because I happened to be standing next to the oven, I could take a peek inside.

But nothing doing.

Before I could even rise from the table to try out my diversionary, water-drinking tactic, she reached over, gently plucked my forearm, and gave me a cheerful wink.

"Come on, let's go get comfortable. Let's have some tea and read a little more. Our biscuits still have a few more minutes."

*Thank you, Lord, for letting her remember about those bis-
cuits. And if it's not too much trouble, pleasepleaseplease remind
her to take them out of the oven before they burn.*

I loved reading the Bible with Mrs. Simpson—and I
loved the feeling of being led by the hand into her dimly lit
parlor. After settling me into my favorite chair, she ambled
slowly but surely toward the china cabinet. A few seconds
later, she was shuffling back, deftly carrying two delicate
teacups and matching saucers. She set them down gently,
each of them on their own fancy doily. Raindrops spattered
against the windows. We were settling in to read.

Her parlor was sheer glory. In my seven-year-old mind at
least, I remember lace coverlets on every chair. Handmade
doilies on each table, most crocheted by Mrs. Simpson herself (some of them were even made by her grandmother,
about a thousand years ago). In the far corner, a walnut-
stained curio cabinet filled with antique trinkets and crystal
baubles. As we sipped on our Lipton tea, she read to me
from the book of Psalms. It was funny, the way it always
happened: somehow, the woman seemed to know precisely
which biblical passages to read at precisely the right time,
and she always centered them around whatever seemed to
be moving in my heart or troubling my mind. She was trying to send me a message that day, as we sat together in her
parlor: to be patient with Sheila, and to rely on God for an
answer on how to deal with the conflict between us. I tried

hard to concentrate on her words, which, at that moment, were from Psalms 27:14 ("Wait on the Lord: be of good courage, and He shall strengthen thine heart: wait, I say, on the Lord.")—but the smell of the biscuits took over my mind, my heart, and my nose. I knew they'd be ready soon. Either that, or burned to a sad and sorrowful crisp.

After a time, we got up and, hand in hand, slowly made our way back to the kitchen. She leaned down to check the oven, smiling to herself. Her smile revealed great news:

It must be eating time!

I watched, mesmerized, as she spread both butter and her homemade peach preserves over each piping-hot biscuit. Before she could even bring the plate over to the table, I was reaching for them. Simultaneously, I heard Mother's inner voice whispering in my ear: *"Don't be rude, Beauty. Take your time when you eat—and always, always leave a little something on your plate when you're finished with your meal. Don't ever become a member of the Clean Plate Club! It's not ladylike to gobble up every crumb. Gobble, gobble. You're not a turkey!"*

I want to tell you that those biscuits melted in my mouth—and I ate about seven of them. I could feel the beginnings of nausea rumbling around in my lower stomach, but I convinced myself it was because I was troubled about Sheila. Mother would have stuck needles in her eyes if she'd known her baby girl was across the street digging into that plate of biscuits with the force of a John Deere bull-dozer. But Mother didn't have to know, now, did she?

Suddenly, I was up on Mrs. Simpson's lap again. I couldn't contain myself. My arms had to hug her. My heart had to thank her. My words had to reassure her: "I love you so much, Mrs. Simpson. The biscuits were heavenly. Thank you so very, very much for going through all that trouble to make them especially for me." I felt better after I'd said it, but she looked a little taken aback.

Then, as if it were an afterthought, I remembered this:

"And I know you always pray for me, Mrs. Simpson. I want to tell you how much I appreciate that, and I want you to know that I pray for you, too. I ask God to take care of you, 'cause I worry about your falling down the steps or choking on your boiled chicken or maybe getting stuck in your bathtub or something. That's why I pray for God to protect you. I don't want anything to happen to you." *Drat! I was suddenly near tears. Wimp!*

She blinked rapidly for a second or two, then quickly licked her top lip; a sure sign that what I'd just said went straight to her heart.

"Well now, you just come here, child," she said in a whisper.

I moved again into her outstretched arms, happy beyond belief to be in her arms.

"It makes me so happy that you keep me in your prayers,"

she said softly. "And it makes me happier even still that you pray on a regular basis."

I smiled softly, eyes downcast. My jumper was almost dry, I noticed. I wondered whether the dirty rainwater from the street (from when the car splashed me) would leave a stain.

Mrs. Simpson wanted to say something else, so I turned my mind away from my jumper and toward my beautiful friend.

"Remember this, too, sweetie: Although I am so deeply touched that you pray for me—and I don't want you to stop!—remember also that prayer is not just about asking for what you want so much as it is silencing your small voice to listen to the Supreme Voice that dwells inside and all around every one of us."

I was pretty sure I understood what she'd just said about not just asking God for what we want when we pray (Mother and Daddy had taught me this, too), but I was more than a little puzzled when she said the part about "silencing my small voice." Was she trying to tell me—in a way that wouldn't hurt my feelings—that I yammered a little too much and that people were starting to get sick and tired of my incessant chatter? Is that what she'd meant by "silencing my own voice"? I didn't learn until years later that by "creating silence" she meant just that: the intentional, sustained effort to silence one's soul for quiet contemplation and to listen for—and actually *hear*—the voice of God when He speaks to us.

She kissed the top of my head and nodded briskly toward the parlor. "Now come on. Let's get back to our reading. We've kept the good Lord waiting long enough, what with the biscuit making and all. It's His time now."

As we were making our way back into the parlor, one big fat biscuit crumb fell from my plate onto the kitchen floor. Thank goodness she was walking in front of me, snapping her dishrag as we moved through the hallway. Faster than a jumping jackrabbit, I picked up the crumb from the floor, kissed it up to God, then popped the buttery morsel into my mouth. I wasn't worried about catching the cooties because (1) I'd kissed it up to God and (2) Mrs. Simpson had the cleanest, shiniest kitchen floor I'd ever seen in my life—skittering dust bunnies and all.

In the parlor again, we repositioned ourselves, automatically selecting our favorite chairs: hers, an overstuffed green arm chair with handmade lace arm covers crocheted by her grandmother; and mine, a deep, wine-colored wing chair that surrounded my little head like a protective friend. I felt safe in the chair. I loved its musty old smell. There was a television in the room, but we rarely watched it when we were together. Once I watched *The Wizard of Oz* on it because I could see it "in color." Well, by "color" I mean that her husband, before he died, had attached one of those red, green, and yellow pieces of plastic over the screen, which meant, by definition, that they were the proud owners of a color TV.

She was as focused as a laser beam. All she wanted to do was read to me from the Bible.

She cleared her throat and began to read aloud in her strong, throaty voice, from Romans 8:38–39. Every word she spoke reminded me that, no matter how bad things got or how mean people became, nothing—but *nothing*—could get in the way of the infinite and everlasting love that God and I had between us. And Mrs. Simpson was right about what she'd said earlier: I *should* be praying for Sheila instead of sending her nasty thoughts.

Slowly, I rose and went over to kneel at her lap. I knew she wanted to pray, and I knew I wanted to as well. We clasped hands and lowered our heads. This time, she lowered her voice to a whisper, as if God himself were standing there right beside us. I lowered my head, too, and clamped my eyes so tightly shut I could have made myself go blind. (I resisted the urge to cross my fingers and scrunch my toes, just in case God didn't believe in all that silliness.)

This was indeed an important prayer: Even though she'd been mean, she was still my friend—and I wanted my friend back. No matter how pigheaded and obstinate we'd both been, I didn't want to be angry anymore. I missed Sheila, and I didn't like it that we were mad at each over a silly banana bike and cruel name-calling.

"Father God," Mrs. Simpson petitioned, "we praise You and uplift Your holy name. I ask You right now, Father, to let Miss Kriss know that she was made in your image, and that she is a wonderful girl with a good, strong brain and a pure, loving heart. Remove those shadows of self-doubt that sometimes surround her, Lord, and guide the two girls back toward the light of friendship and forgiveness. Lead them and guide them toward the truth. Toward Your truth—which is the only Truth there is."

My eyes were clamped tight, of course, but I sure was tempted to open them for a quick peek at Mrs. Simpson, just to see what she was doing with her face and all. I wanted to see her expression, 'cause her voice was beginning to sound kind of like she was about to cry. She finished with a flourish, raising her hands toward the ceiling.

"Amen!" she whispered, hands still uplifted above her.

"Amen," I repeated softly, lifting my hands in the air as well (even though it felt awkward because I didn't know what to do with them up there like that).

"Amen!" we finished in unison.

I felt better already. Less bony. A tad more graceful.

She studied me for a moment, trying to make sure I was listening. After a minute more, she spoke: "I hope you don't go thinking that the amount of friends you have makes you the person you are—cause if you do, you're just dead *wrong*, honey!"

I must have looked confused, because she continued on: "What I'm trying to say, baby, is that you don't need a certain number of friends—only a number of friends you can be certain of!" I liked that one, too, and vowed to memorize it and pull it out when I was older. *You don't need a certain number of friends; only a number of friends you can be certain of.* Good stuff, indeed.

On that rainy afternoon, with my full stomach and renewed spirit, it was Mrs. Simpson who'd shown me the clear path. The path without the bumps or the anger or the jealousy—and let's face it, I had been a little envious of Sheila's new bike, pure and simple. Plus, I was angry at the name she'd called me, but already I felt that anger melting away like butter on a piping-hot scratch biscuit. I felt renewed. Hopeful. And infinitely thankful to my friend Mrs. Luella Rae Simpson.

Taking a final sip of tea, she wiped both of the cups and the dainty saucers clean with her ever-present dish towel, then she handed them over to me in a neatly stacked, precarious little pile. Because she was trembling slightly, the dishes made little rattling sounds as she held them in her outstretched hand.

"These are for you," she said without fanfare or ceremony. "You know I don't even take them out unless you come over, so I figured you'd probably get more use out of them than me—you know, for when you're older and start attending fancy tea parties and Garden Club meetings." *What in the world is a "Garden Club meeting"? I know that Aunt Bee sits on the Board of Directors of hers—along with Clara and all the other Fine Ladies of Mayberry—but how does this pertain to me? What do the Garden Club Ladies actually do in Detroit (as opposed to Mayberry)? Are they glorious Lipton tea–drinking ladies who sit cross-legged in their pretty gardens, laughing and talking among the neat rows of collard greens and tomatoes?*

Hot tears sprang to my eyes before I could stop them. She might have been old, but she had eyes like a hawk. Even in her shadowy parlor, she saw the shine of my tears immediately.

"Don't go getting all fussy on me now, chil'. It's just a couple of old cups and a few saucers. Not even a full set. Just put them away for safekeeping till you're ready to use them. And when you finally do use them, think of me."

Right then and there, I pledged to take good care of her beautiful teacups—maybe I could even save them long enough until I became a real woman with a real family, when we would sip on tea every Sunday afternoon after church.

After some time, she patted the arm of her chair, indicating it was time for her to rise. She said she had to "fetch something" from upstairs. About two thousand hours later, she came back downstairs, dish towel in her left hand, a carefully folded, yellowed piece of paper in another. Reaching the bottom of the stairs and slightly winded, she handed me the piece of paper.

"My mother gave me this a long, long time ago, after I'd had a disagreement with a girl, Billie Jean Watkins, who lived on the property next to ours."

She watched me watching her.

"Go ahead; unfold it. Read it, nice and loud so I can hear it again," she instructed, still standing there with her dish towel. "My mama gave it to me, and I'm asking you to read it out loud, 'cause it sounds like you need to hear it. Now read!"

The woman could certainly be bossy when she wanted to.

I carefully unfolded the note, studying the writer's neat penmanship.

"Think about your friend Sheila when you read it," was her last instruction.

I cleared my throat, ready to obey and perform for my friend:

> If I knew you and you knew me,
> And each of us could clearly see,
> By that inner life divine,
> The meaning of your heart and mine;
> I'm sure that we would differ less
> And clasp our hands in friendliness,
> If you knew me, and I knew you.

I looked up at her, worried that I'd mispronounced most of the words (at the time I still wasn't a proficient reader), but she was already shuffling toward the sunroom, rummaging around for something else. A busybody, she was. Finally, she pulled out a small brown paper bag, offering it to me with kind, tired eyes. Realizing that she was offering the bag for me to take home my teacups in, I made a mad dash into her kitchen and swiped the nearest hand towel I could find. I whizzed back into the sunroom.

"I'll bring your towel back, Mrs. Simpson. I promise I will," I mumbled as I wrapped the china safely inside the towel's folds. Before I knew it, my brown bag was full of treats.

My very own china.

And about seven or eight scratch biscuits Mrs. Simpson had wrapped earlier for me to take back to my family. (I could still feel their warmth though the aluminum foil.)

It had been a wonderful visit.

As I crossed the street on my way back home, Mrs. Simpson stood on her front porch and hollered out one last Holy reminder. As usual, she'd hollered out precisely what I needed to hear, precisely when I needed to hear it:

"Remember what it says in Proverbs 17:17, sweetness!"

Did that mean I'd have to look it up in our Bible when I got home? Shoot! Cookie and I were going to catch bumblebees in Miss Marla's backyard garden! And I knew it because I could see the

mason jars already lined up on the top step of her porch, with
holes punched into the lid of each jar so the bees could breathe.

As if reading my mind, Mrs. Simpson recited the verse
while she was standing on her porch. I have to admit, it was
the first time in my life I'd ever heard Scripture being hollered by a hundred-and-fifty-year-old woman.

"It says, 'A friend loveth at all times!'"

Now, *that* was a good one. *A friend loveth at all times?* Just
hearing the words calmed my soul and softened my heart.

At that moment, the rain stopped. The sun didn't suddenly start shining and the birds didn't suddenly begin
chirping or anything that dramatic, but the rain did stop,
which I took to be a divine miracle or a spiritual sign or
something.

Turns out it was.

In that next moment, I heard the unmistakable swish
of her bicycle tires before I saw the shine of her face. Sheila
rode past me, colored streamers flying from her handlebars.

"I like your new bike. It's sure pretty," I said simply.

She slowed down and glanced back at me, surprised and
pleased. And then, the six magic words that made me feel all
right with God and Mrs. Simpson and everybody in the
whole wide world: "You wanna ride it some time?"

Sheila was offering me a ride on her fancy bike! I guessed
we were friends again. I felt like clapping and hopping up

and down in relief, but that wouldn't have been cool. Instead, I just smiled and reached out to hold her hand.

After a brief moment, I looked straight into her eyes and spoke quietly, calling her by her nickname out of pure habit. "I'm sorry, She-She. I don't know exactly what happened to make us so mad at each other, but I sure would like it if we could be friends again."

I waited, holding my breath, praying that she wouldn't reject my apology. If something wicked or cruel-hearted had come out of her mouth at that point, when I was at my most vulnerable, I'd have probably smacked the taste out of her mouth. Or knocked her into next week. Or snatched her baldheaded.

But she didn't.

"What're *you* sorry for, girl?" Her face told me she was sincere; she honestly couldn't figure it out. "Shoot, *I'm* the one who called you a 'skinny-legged beanpole'!" She kicked her front tire in disgust. "I should be apologizing to *you*!"

Another brief moment of silence, then she spoke again.

"Girl, you *know* you're not a beanpole, right?" she asked with only a hint of a grin on her face.

"Of *course* I know that, She-She," I answered, fighting the urge to pull at my fuzzy pigtail. "I figured you were just in a bad mood about something else." *Why was I minimizing all of this, when it had been weighing on my mind for days on end? What a coward.*

"You know why I called you that?" she asked, casting a furtive glance up and the down the street, as though she was worried that someone else might be listening.

She'd piqued my curiosity. In the back of my mind, I wondered if Mrs. Simpson was still standing on her porch, watching us become friends again. If she was, I knew she'd be smiling and praising God and thanking Him for answering her prayers. But I dared not turn around to look. This time belonged to me and Sheila.

She answered her own question.

"Because my sister called me that same name the day Mama and Daddy gave me this here new bike," she said, tapping the handlebars lightly. "I mean, she really screamed it, too. I'm surprised you didn't hear her big mouth."

I might have been mean at times, but I was never ever *cruel*—and to call your own sister a skinny-legged beanpole was just plain mean. It was sinful and downright cruel. In all of my seven long years of living, not one of my six siblings had ever said anything mean or bad to me. All I *ever* received from them was love—pure, unconditional, uncomplicated love. I felt tears stinging my eyes; tears for poor Sheila, who had a sister mean as a junkyard dog. (I'd heard tell that she used to pull the legs off spiders and fry ants on the hot asphalt with a magnifying glass.)

I tried to comfort my friend.

"She's just jealous 'cause you got a new bike." (Never

mind that it was *me* who'd been secretly jealous, too!) "She's just mad 'cause her own bike is about five thousand years old and has about two hundred spokes missing, so she can barely ride that old ugly thing."

I could see the beginnings of a smile on Sheila's face, so I continued, praying that my humor would help her hurting heart.

"Her handlebars are so rusty, I wouldn't ride that old bike if she *paid* me!"

Heartened by her grin, I forged ahead.

"Shoot," I said even louder, "my mama might have to take me to the doctor for a tetanoose shot if she found out I'd even *touched* her rusty old, beat-up bike!" (I hadn't mastered the pronunciation of "tetanus" just yet, but my effort was well-intentioned.)

Finally, Sheila laughed. A loud, long laugh that made her double over and clap her hands in glee. I had to reach out to steady her body *and* her bike so that she wouldn't topple over. In that instant, while Sheila was distracted, I took a lightning-fast glimpse toward Mrs. Simpson's house. There she was, standing at the top step of her porch. She'd seen the entire scene, and I prayed her vision was good enough to see that Sheila—at that precise moment—was actually *doubled over in laughter!*

Mrs. Simpson waved a pleasant, happy wave to me from across the street. I could tell by her body language that she was pleased as punch that the two of us had finally made up. I also knew that she was thanking the Lord above for answering her prayers about renewing our friendship. *Whatever you do, Mrs. Simpson, pleasepleaseplease don't start hollering and yelling from across the street. Not in front of Sheila. I'll die a thousand deaths.*

But Mrs. Simpson didn't yell. She just kept waving, more than likely thanking God for reuniting two little girls in friendship. *I* was thanking God, too, while I steadied Sheila as she laughed against her bike that day. And my mind was whirring. How is it that God knows exactly what we need, exactly when we need it? How is it that He answers each and every one of our prayers so faithfully? And how in the Sam Hill is it that, no matter what challenges we face, He never turns His back on us?

After a minute, our laughs turned into happy whimpers, and we straightened up to wipe the tears from our eyes. She looked at me again, forcibly trying to repress another gale of laughter.

"Her handlebars sure are rusty, aren't they?" Sheila asked through happy tears.

"Rustier than her rusty old knees when she forgets to put on the Jergens after her bath!" I answered, on a roll now.

And with that, both of us doubled over into laughter yet again, letting Sheila's fancy new banana bike drop gently onto the grass in front of my house. The more she laughed, the harder I laughed.

Not only was our laughter contagious, but our friendship was contagious, too, because about two or three minutes later, good ol' Cookie came bounding off her porch to join us in the fun. She didn't even know what we were laughing at—and we couldn't even explain it to her because we were laughing so hard—but by sheer virtue of the fact that the three of us were fast friends, she assumed it must have been hilarious. So there we sat on my front lawn, the three of us laughing like hyenas—then laughing even harder once we stood up to discover that our backsides were soaked to the bone. (We'd all forgotten that the grass was still wet from the rain.)

A minute later, though, a familiar sound stunned all of us into sudden silence. We froze in our positions, listening. Attentive.

There it was again!

Instinctively, and without uttering so much as a word, we each sprinted off in different directions, running like the wind toward our own homes. Seconds later, we came together again, armed with the coins we needed. And as fast as three jumping jackrabbits, we tore down the street to catch that ol' ice-cream man before he turned the corner.

◆

NEEDLESS to say, the treasures that Mrs. Simpson gave me that day are still dear to me. My friend had shared with me a piece of her past that she deemed precious and perhaps even irreplaceable. Two beautiful teacups, each filled with the memories of the countless warm, shining summer afternoons that Mrs. Simpson and I spent together. Whether it was reading from the Good Book, rocking together on her front porch, or sipping hot Lipton tea in her parlor, it was really our love that sustained us.

So thank you, Mrs. Simpson, as I magnify your memory. Thank you for nudging me toward the joy and relief and freedom that comes from leading a spiritual life. Thank you for helping me become God-centered and filled with faith— not with fear—and for showering me with the powerful reminder that *none* of us is perfect; and for that reason, we are not free to judge others. We must only show compassion and forgiveness. At all times.

And today, sweet friend of mine, your precious teacups remain perfectly intact—generations later. Not a mark or a scratch or a chip. And I know that, even now, as you look down on me today, you're shaking your head in quiet pride—pride that your fine, fuzzy-haired, seven-year-old friend grew into a memory-maker who's able to sidestep the constraints of time and place, and travel way, way back to those golden, sun-splashed days of her childhood.

A Forever Box holds sweet, sentimental trinkets and interesting baubles, of course, but it also exists as a way to remind us to hold fast to the friendships of our past as well. If handled with care, our loving relationships with those long since departed can live forever. The powerful joy that comes with pure friendship can live on indefinitely. And when we preserve and pass down those beautiful trinkets and treasures from a special friendship, we help validate the fact that that person made a lasting, significant difference on this earth, and it reminds us that their earthly presence counted for something big and bold and beautiful.

Today, Mrs. Simpson is gone. My father is no longer alive, either. But fortunately for me, the love I have for both of them is boundless and unforgettable. And whenever I hold the teacups that Mrs. Simpson gave me on that wonderfully rainy afternoon, I am reminded of God's infinite wisdom, his glorious grace, and his tender loving kindness. I am reminded that, if we are to hear the voice of our Higher Power, then we must still our bodies and silence our minds. I am reminded that we are here to love, not to judge. To show compassion, not cruelty.

Without a doubt, it was Mrs. Luella Rae Simpson (along with my parents) who helped teach me about the enduring, everlasting power of prayer. The simple act of holding one of her teacups in my hand reminds me all over again that our prayers are heard, they are answered, and they provide us a direct, sustained way to communicate with our Creator—whatever Creator it is that we choose to worship.

When I look at my china, I think of you, Mrs. Simpson, and the warm memories we will always share.

My heart is filled with gladness.

And every time I remember our summer days, kind friend, these Biblical words come to mind: *My cup runneth over.*

IN PRAISE OF PUMPS

❦

B Y THE FOLLOWING morning, it was raining cats and dogs again, making this the third day of steady downpour. The neighbors stood outside on their porches, peeking up at the sky and chattering to one another about the "Forty Days and Forty Nights" Bible story of nonstop rain, but I wasn't really worried. A quick peek out the front door told me that the gutters on our street were not yet clogged, and the rainwater hadn't yet risen above the curb—which it did sometimes during heavy storms. So I figured if ol' Noah could survive, then we could, too.

This summer day, I was embarking on yet another mission, and I had every intention of accomplishing it before the sun went down. But for *this* particular mission, I was going to have to enlist a little bit of Mother's help. I wanted to get down the street to see Miss Miriam, because we hadn't visited in more than two weeks and I was just a little worried about her, what with the nasty weather and all.

There were a couple of challenges to this mission: Unlike Mrs. Simpson, who lived across the street, Miss Miriam lived farther down the block. I was no scaredy-cat, mind you, but from my seven-year-old perspective, her large, looming house looked a little spooky. There might be monsters. Plus, it was a rare thing for me to walk so far from home by myself. I wasn't being a little-girlie-baby, by any means. It's just that I generally stayed within very, very close proximity to our house. I felt uncomfortable straying too far. But friendship called, and something deep inside told me that Miss Miriam really wanted me to visit.

So I sidled up to Mother, who was busy unpacking groceries and arranging the canned green beans "just so" in our cupboard.

"I'm worried about Miss Miriam," I told her in an urgent whisper. "I sure would like to go down to her house for a visit, but it's raining too hard and you know I lost my Bozo the Clown umbrella last week, so I can't really walk by myself." *Hint, hint.*

Mother stopped momentarily, grimacing at a dented can of Green Giant sweet peas. (She *hated* dented vegetable cans because she thought they gave off salmonella or cooties or some kind of lethal, liquid poison that seeps into the vegetables from the inside of the can.)

Finally, she looked down at me, rolling the dented can of peas around and around in her hand. I could tell she was considering taking the can back to A&P to see if she could either get a refund or a new, non-dented can. Sweet Mother. She could get quite salty when it came to protecting her children. Our health and well-being were her top priorities, and she'd do anything to keep us away from danger—in this particular case, away from potentially spoiled food that might kill us or make us sick. Finally, she focused on me.

"I guess I could walk you over," she said slowly, her eyebrows furrowed as she studied the can again. (She was *really* worried about that dented can of peas.)

"Run, get your rain boots from the hall and I'll meet you on the porch. We'll take Daddy's big umbrella. I'll call Miss Miriam on our way out the door to let her know you're coming."

I loved Daddy's big black umbrella. I felt so safe underneath, and I never ever got wet when we used it. That thing was huge, with about a thousand spokes underneath to hold it up nice and wide, and it had a thick wooden handle shaped like a J. Only an adult could carry it. Only an adult would want to. It was like a magic shield; the best umbrella I'd ever seen.

On the way to Miss Miriam's, I resisted the urge to stomp

through every puddle we passed. Mother wouldn't have liked it one bit, and I didn't want to splash dirty water on her pretty little rain boots. (Mother always wore pretty things, and these rain boots were among my favorites. They were gray, with a black patent leather heel and four black buttons that looked like shiny raisins going up one side and a fancy gray zipper going up the other side. I always thought it was utterly cool that the color of the zipper was gray, to match the boot fabric. Every other zipper I'd ever seen was the ugly, steel-looking color that turned kind of rusty brown after it had been used for a while.)

No, I didn't want to mess up her fancy rain boots. Plus, it would have been kind of rude to walk into Miss Miriam's beautiful home with sopping-wet feet, dripping water and maybe mud all over her shiny, highly polished hardwood floors.

Mother and I arrived at the curb where I would cross the street. Butterflies danced a silly jig in the pit of my stomach. What a girlie-girl. The thought of leaving Mother's side—even for a few minutes—made my stomach hurt. Big baby. I turned and waved a weak and pitiful good-bye, so close to tears that I couldn't speak.

"Call when you're finished, sweetheart, and one of us will come back to this very spot to pick you up!" Mother said, pointing to the curb. "And tell Miss Miriam we all said hello. Send her our best, Beauty."

I hitched up my overalls and turned to look at my mother again. I ignored the ridiculous lump rising in my throat. I just *hated* seeing Mother walk away from me, under any circumstance. But I was on a mission; on my way to visit my beautiful friend. It was time to cross the street.

"Look both ways!" Mother warned as I splashed my way to the other side. I could feel her presence there behind me—standing, watching, making sure I made it safely, probably smiling to herself as she watched her youngest child running zigzag between the raindrops. The moment Mother heard Miss Miriam's squeaky screen door open and slam shut, she knew I was safe. I could imagine her standing there for a moment, then turning to walk back home, mentally preparing to tackle another of a hundred waiting tasks in the busy Clark household.

Once inside, I always hightailed it straight up to Miss Miriam's bedroom, taking two steps at a time. I arrived just outside her bedroom door slightly winded, my heart pounding like crazy. I swear I was a nervous child and quite the worrier, too, for a seven-year-old. I thought I was going into cardiac arrest—or at least feeling the first few, tight wheezes of an oncoming asthma attack. No doubt about it: I was just a tad dramatic.

The moment I entered Miss Miriam's world of sterling-silver hair combs and colored perfume bottles, I was instantly transported to a world of finery and fashion, satin wraps and sequined hats. My name wasn't Kristin anymore. It was Dorothy Dandridge, maybe. Or Lena Horne. Fancy women who shimmied when they walked.

To this day, I still don't know why Miss Miriam spent so much time in her bedroom. Maybe she was sick and elegantly immobile and I was just too young to realize it. I don't even remember who else lived in the house with her, because she was always in her bedroom. Maybe she was a boarder. I simply didn't know. But I *do* know this: I learned to walk in my first pair of high heels when I was seven—and they were *her* heels, bright yellow satin pumps.

She was sitting primly in her vanity chair, studying her cheekbones in the mirror when I entered her room. She didn't exactly smile when she saw me, but I could tell she was happy to see me because her eyes were very bright, and it looked like they were dancing all around. She accepted my hug graciously, even elegantly. By that I mean she didn't even budge from her sitting position when I moved in close to hug her. She just kept sitting there on her little tufted chair, waiting for me to figure out the best way to embrace her—physically, rather awkward, especially if you're trying to give someone a big bear hug. After about thirty seconds, though, she lifted her face ever so slightly and turned her right cheek toward me so that I could kiss it. Kind of like how the movie stars do it. Or Queen Elizabeth. She was the classiest woman I knew, and I felt lucky to be her friend.

"So what are we going to do today?" she asked through a thin smile, holding her left hand up close so she could inspect her fingernails. Needless to say, her nails were always immaculate and her "cuticle beds"—as she called them—were never torn or ragged. Miss Miriam was definitely not a nail-biter. She was way too classy for such nonsense. She once told me that the secret to keeping healthy, neat-looking nails was to massage the cuticles gently, immediately after you've washed your hands, while the skin is still soft. Unfortunately I could never remember to do this because my hands were just always so *busy*. Who had time for proper cuticle care? I'd rather be using my hands to draw giant *X*'s on the sidewalk in front of our house with a piece of thick, white chalk so that Cookie and I could play hopscotch or Mother-May-I until the streetlights came on. Or making mud pies—sloppy, dripping pies, sometimes with pebbles in them—that we'd let "bake" simply by leaving them in the hot sun all day, in neat little rows along the bottom step of Cookie's back porch. No sirree, at that young age, my hands were busy doing other things that were much more fun than cuticle massage. I did promise myself, though, to either remember the manicure tip for when I grew up, or to pass this wisdom along to my older sisters. (I ended up doing both.)

But on this day, I had an idea. I'd been thinking about it for a little while, and if anybody on God's green earth could do it, it would certainly be Miss Miriam. For some reason, I felt embarrassed about blurting it out, but she *had* asked what I wanted to do that day, so I thought I may as well spill the beans.

"I'd sure like to learn to walk in high-heel shoes one of these old days," I said as demurely—and evasively—as possible. I didn't want it to seem like I was *demanding* to learn at that precise moment. I was trying to make it sound almost like an afterthought, rather than a plea. She saw right through it immediately.

"So is the direct answer to my direct question that you'd like for me to *teach* you to walk in high-heel shoes?"

Heavens to Betsy! My elderly friends were the loves of my life, but they didn't believe in pussyfooting around when it came to communicating. Maybe they sensed that they didn't have much longer on this earth anyway, and for that reason alone they might as well just get straight to the point in every conversation. They certainly must have realized that their body clocks were tick-tick-ticking. Shoot, if I was a hundred years old, I probably wouldn't waste any time getting straight to the point, either—especially if I knew it could literally be a day or even a minute before I had to leave this earth to go and meet my Maker. No, I couldn't blame her one bit for her directness—but it did make her seem kind of brash and intimidating. (It dawned on me, later in my life, that Miss Miriam probably wasn't quite as prehistoric as I'd originally thought . . . but at the time, it felt to me like she was old enough to have walked through the Garden of Eden right alongside Adam and Eve and the serpent and all.)

"Well, yes, I would like to learn," I answered, feeling a little silly. I wondered if another fuzzy tendril of my hair had popped free. Miss Miriam was the queen of propriety and fashion, and it wouldn't have sat well with her if my hair had been popping out all over the place. I patted my head self-consciously, trying to adjust my two pigtails. She observed this, of course, and just *had* to comment.

"Your pigtails are absolutely adorable, sweet thing." (She used words like *absolutely adorable* because of her classiness, I think. If anyone else had said it, it would have sounded stilted and fake and too over-the-top. But coming from Miss Miriam, it was a super-supreme compliment, and I felt my self-confidence inflate just the tiniest bit.)

So I forged ahead, newly confident.

"Thank you, Miss Miriam. And yes, I would very much like you to teach me to walk in high-heeled shoes. But only if you feel up to it."

She eyed me carefully, the hint of a smile on her face.

"Well, it's about *time* you asked! I was actually beginning to worry. Here you are, seven going on eight, and you still can't navigate in a pair of heels. You know you can't splash around in those horrid plastic rain boots and your scuffed Keds for the rest of your life, Chipper. Now let's get this show on the road!"

Wow! What an uncharacteristic outburst of enthusiasm—especially from prim-and-proper Miss Miriam! But her comment was kind of a backhanded insult, too. I didn't know whether to feel offended by her comment about my "horrid" rain boots and "scuffed" Keds or not. Somehow, because I knew her so well, I just had to assume that she hadn't meant to bruise my tender little ego. She simply wanted me to join her in her fine, fine world of fashion. And I was happy to be recruited.

She stood up and walked toward a huge armoire. (I think I remember it being even taller than she was.) She opened its doors to reveal a column of shoe boxes, each box label-side-out and stacked neatly atop one another. It might have been my overactive imagination, but I'm pretty sure I spied several fancy dresses in there. Some sequined gowns. I thought I even saw a feathered boa toward the back, but I didn't want to gawk.

Peering into the armoire, Miss Miriam carefully inspected her inventory. After a few seconds, she selected one special shoe box and yanked it out crisply, as expertly as any shoe saleslady.

"These will do for now," she said with what I could hear was mounting excitement in her voice. Classy or not, *this* lady was getting all revved up about our upcoming Fashion Extravaganza.

She opened the box with a bit of ceremony, removing

two magnificent satin pumps. Thrusting them in my direction, she directed me to go sit on the bed to remove my Keds. (My "horrid" Keds, as she'd called them.) In those days, most children wore shoes inside their rain boots just because it was practical, but it always felt a little ungainly to me. Still, Mother insisted, so that was the way it had to be. I had to wear both the shoe *and* the boot.

Feeling slightly self-conscious and praying to Jesus that my damp feet wouldn't stink up her bedroom to high heaven, I sat on the edge of her bed and set my feet free. I sat completely still for a moment, just to see if I could smell my own feet stinking up the room. I would have died a thousand deaths. Miss Miriam liked the smell of *French perfume* and *scented talcum powder*—not the neighbor girl's smelly, rain-soaked feet.

But if she smelled anything, she didn't let on. She was just excited. And then, before I knew it, her pumps were on my feet!

"Now stand up, Krissy. Stand up and take your first steps!"

Her voice had grown slightly louder, which told me she was happy to be so fully engaged in this fashion fiesta.

I wiggled this way and wobbled that way as I walked, but Miss Miriam's bejeweled hands held my skinny arms steady as she patiently, urgently whispered instructions into the perfumed air around us with ladylike finesse:

"You're not charging the Red Brigade in those shoes, honey pie! You have to take teeny-tiny steps. Don't ever rush yourself when you're all dressed up—even if your feet are killing you. *Don't ever rush*. Remember that! Ladies don't hurry. Go slow; take your sweet time. And when you're wearing high heels, learn to balance yourself from inside the tips of your toes, not on the balls of your feet."

Inside the tips of my toes? What in the devil does that mean? Where can one actually locate the "inside" of the tip of a toe?

I didn't dare ask.

After a few minutes of teetering around, we both sat back down on her bed. I felt luxurious. I think I even tipped my nose up into the air slightly, like a famous movie star. I'd walked in my first pair of heels! Go tell it on the mountain! I was now, officially, a little lady.

I gently removed her pumps from my feet, proud as a peacock and feeling very grown-up, taking special care to return both shoes back to their tissue-papered box. I resisted the urge to rub my aching toes. Dorothy or Lena would never have done that. Instead, I tied my Keds back up and walked over to her vanity table as gracefully as I could manage.

"My ma says to tell you hello," I said, fingering one of her ornate, sterling-silver hair combs on her table. What did the women of yesterday do with their hair to avoid flyaway frizzies, especially in the rain and humidity? I tugged self-consciously at my own fuzzy tendrils.

"Your mother is an angel," said Miss Miriam definitively, moving back to her vanity table and gently pushing me off her chair so that she could sit down. "And she's as smart as the dickens—all of you Clark women are. Tell her I send my love, too, honey. That woman is a jewel; smart as a whip, prettier than a bushel of golden apples, and, even after seven children, she's kept her trim figure. It comes as no surprise that she modeled in her younger days, with a figure and a face like that!" *How in the Sam Hill did Miss Miriam know about Mother's modeling days when I only just found out about them myself? Why was I always the last person on earth to find out all the good stuff?*

She continued her praise of Mother.

"When God made her, He threw in all of the right ingredients: brains, beauty, grace, compassion, and humility."

My goodness! Miss Miriam wasn't big on compliments, so I was a bit taken aback by her observations. Pulling me close in so that I stood directly beside her, she picked up a silver hand mirror and held it up so that I could see my face. Then, she picked up one of her antique hair combs and carefully inserted it into my hair. I looked at my reflection, cocking my head ever so slightly, trying to suppress a smile. Until that point in my young life, I'd never worn anything in my hair except for the occasional ribbon or plain bow—and even then it was usually for something like picture day at school or maybe to church on Easter Sunday. An antique comb was a very special thing. I was feeling prouder by the minute.

Holding the mirror closer up to my face, she said to me, "Just look at that beautiful brown face of yours, honey pie."

I looked.

It *was* brown; that much was certain—but I didn't necessarily see beauty in the face that stared back at me. Feeling I needed to respond, I simply smiled weakly and nodded my head. My two pigtails were sticking out so far, the mirror couldn't even capture their entire image.

"There is no greater beauty than a woman who has confidence in herself, who is beautiful from the inside out, and who is comfortable in her own skin," Miss Miriam said. "Too many of us get caught up in the snares of self-pity, powerlessness, and superficial beauty."

What in the world? I thought a "snare" was the contraption with the sharp teeth that would clamp around a bear's paw or a human's foot if they accidentally stepped on it during a walk in the forest. But I guess I'm wrong. Drat. I'll have to look up that word, too! Mel's Bells. I'm gonna spend half my summer with my head stuck in the dictionary.

Miss Miriam prattled on about the glorious strengths—and weaknesses—of today's woman. I could tell that the things she was saying were probably right on target, but she had kind of a bad habit of using words that were too big; too big for a seven-year-old, that's for sure.

"And although I'm far too old to do it, little women like you will one day soon evolve into full-fledged adults, and *that's* when you can do your part to help nudge your sisters— *all* of them, black and white, young and old—nudge them toward a place where they're treated with respect, paid as much at their jobs as the men they work with, and looked upon as equals in this unequal society of ours."

It sounded like a lot of work.

Miss Miriam's words didn't really resonate with me until years later, after I'd transitioned into what she called "a full-fledged adult." Without a doubt, she was a woman ahead of her time. She was the modern-day Gloria Steinem—with a slightly better sense of fashion.

"Did you get your cookies on your way up?" Miss Miriam asked. She was examining her cheekbones in the mirror again, but this time she turned her face sideways in an effort to get a glimpse of her profile, which looked kind of funny, but I dared not laugh.

I didn't have the heart to tell her that I was usually too frightened to stop in her kitchen—especially when thunder was rumbling outside and her glass windows were rattling like madmen all over the place.

"No," I answered, fighting back another lie. "I'm not really hungry, and we're probably going to be eating pretty soon after I get home."

In that moment, I tried to visualize Miss Miriam eating

dinner. Did she eat by herself? Did she actually walk down to the kitchen and eat at the kitchen table? Or did she eat in her bedroom? Who cooked? I somehow couldn't imagine my glamorous woman-friend bending down low into the oven to check on her homemade scratch biscuits like Mrs. Simpson did—that kind of thing definitely wouldn't ring her bell. I did hope that she had someone else to eat with, though. I hated the thought of her eating in that big kitchen all by herself.

I also had something else on my mind, and I needed to get it off my chest.

"Miss Miriam?" I asked, wishing God would send me a sign if what I was about to ask was out of order or inappropriate for a seven-year-old to be asking a two-hundred-year-old lady.

"Yes, you sweet thing, what is it?"

"Does thunder scare you?"

I didn't know if it was considered disrespectful to be asking such things of an old and elegant woman, but we were *friends*—and true friendship knew no borders or boundaries.

It was a legitimate question, about the thunder. I wondered—and worried—about her sleeping alone in that big old bed of hers, probably sitting up at night with her sheets held up to her chin, her teeth chattering and all, frightened of the nighttime noises outside. I loved Miss Miriam, and I definitely didn't want her to be scared—of thunder or anything else.

She smiled, smoothing her red velvet robe. I thought of Miss Simpson and the faded old dish towel she carried around with her constantly, and of me and Mother sitting on the sofa talking about racial dignity and the power of pride. How lucky I was to have these three miraculous ladies in my life! My heart grew so large with love for all of them that I thought it might open up and burst. Each of these women were so different, yet so much the same. And each of them loved me more than pancakes or the color pink. More than waffle cones or water fights with Cookie. Even more than candy apples or Captain Kangaroo!

But my question about thunder still lingered between us. For some reason, it was important to me that I know she wasn't scared.

She took her time answering. (As I knew from my high-heel-walking lesson, she was *not* a woman to be rushed.) Her eyes looked a little dreamy.

"Sometimes at night, when the thunder gives a great clap like it did last night, I sit bolt upright in bed and look all around, like something's going to jump right out of my closet. Last night, a tree branch scraped against my window and I just about had a heart attack.

"'Who on God's green earth is prowling around in my backyard?' I actually said out loud. Thank the Lord above that no one actually *answered* me, little one, or I really would have fainted dead away. Oh yes, child. I was scared. That ol' storm was loud enough to rattle my windows, and I was praying to the dickens that all that wind and rain wouldn't rip out my hydrangeas."

So typical of her. Selfless. Classy. Unaffected. Praying for the safety of her hydrangeas more urgently than praying for her own personal safety. I loved her in large, gulping doses.

"Why do you ask, baby? Did last night's storm scare you?"

"Yes, ma'am, it scared me pretty bad. I heard that same thunderclap you did, and it scared me so bad I . . . I . . ." And here I hesitated because what I was about to say was definitely, well, unladylike. *Indelicate*.

"That you *what*, child?" she prodded, sounding a little impatient. "Speak your piece. You know you don't have to hold your tongue with me."

". . . that I peed the bed," I answered honestly, feeling a great burden lifted from my shoulders. (She'd *asked*, hadn't she?)

Mother hadn't even been angry when it happened, either. All she'd done was fish around in the upstairs linen closet for some fresh sheets, had my sister Noelle wipe me down with a warm, soapy washcloth in our green bathtub, and asked my other sister Nikki to put the new sheets on the bed. I loved my older siblings with a furious force—and they loved me right back, surrounding me with light and laughter from the moment I was born, and ever since. I felt blessed and smiled upon that we were such a close-knit group. They, along with Mother and Daddy and God, were the center of my life.

Still, there was the matter of the little *accident* with my overactive bladder. I tried not to feel embarrassed, and I deeply regretted having used the word *peed* in my conversation with Miss Miriam. Even Mother scowled at words like that because she considered them crude.

But Miss Miriam only nodded sympathetically. "You're certainly not the first child to"—and here, she cleared her throat and pursed her lips slightly as though she'd just sucked on a slice of a bitter lemon—"*wet* the bed during the night, and you certainly won't be the last. Don't give it another thought. For a child your age, I'm afraid you might just worry yourself a little too much. There'll be enough of life to live—and worry about—later, once you're good and grown. For now, play hide-and-seek. Eat ice cream cones. Pull the dandelions out of Mr. Dewey's front lawn and give them to your mother as a beautiful bouquet. Enjoy your life, because before you know it, you'll be my age!"

Two hundred years old? Will I still have my banana bike?

She continued, "Yes, yes, enjoy life while you're still young, so that when you *do* eventually grow old like me, you won't have any regrets—because by then, honey, it'll be too late."

She continued giving me advice about the future and the world around us. Everything she said sounded wise—but I couldn't quite absorb all the larger life lessons she was talking about, using all those big words. So I just nodded and hoped that I *looked like* I understood.

"As you grow into a young lady, honey pie, hold fast to the indisputable truth that it's us women who hold the keys to unlocking the secrets of this world around us. The men are the hunters and the gatherers—which is important, of course—but *we* are the nurturers. The protectors! The ones who watch, and listen and learn. We are the ones who create that universal magnetic field, to which everyone is instinctively drawn. Yes sirree, Bob. We still have a lot of work to do—but who in the Sam Hill says we can't be beautiful and well-dressed while we're doing it?" (She laughed a little when she said that last part; I think she thought it was kind of clever.)

I kept listening, getting the gist of her message about how women are so powerful and all, but I was still a little confused. *Did the word* nurturer *have anything to do with loving nature? If that's the case, I could be counted as a "woman," too, 'cause I liked camping out and walking in the woods at Belle Isle and canoeing at Palmer Park as much as the next woman did! Hot diggity! Miss Miriam must think that I'm a woman, too!*

I smiled as she spoke, glowing and newly confident in my new womanhood. She continued:

"Today's women—women of the '60s—have both power *and* beauty. We've come a long way, sweetie. Not all that long ago, women couldn't even vote. Why, I wouldn't even be surprised if one day—certainly not in my lifetime and probably not in yours—the people of this country even elected a female president! Why, honey, if you let your imagination *really* run all over Robin's red barn, this world may one day even see a black man in the White House! What we have to do is have *faith*, honey! Faith in God, and in the uncompromising belief that He knows what we *want*—but he gives us what we *need*!"

She was really getting excited now. I kind of hoped she hadn't forgotten about our high-heel-walking lesson.

Miss Miriam's predictions about a female or a black man as president, though, had really started me thinking. I thought about her words. Could I imagine a woman or a black man in the White House? It was a difficult question for a seven-year-old growing up in the mid-'60s. Still, my answer was a resounding *yep*. For just a quick flash of a minute, sitting there in Miss Miriam's spacious bedroom, I let my imagination run a few gallops ahead of my mind. Who could I see in the White House besides . . . well . . . a white male? I could certainly picture someone as dignified as, say, Martin Luther King Jr., sitting behind his big fancy desk in the Oval Office, signing important papers and maybe lowering himself to his knees every once in a while, to pray for his country and the world and all. (And was the Oval Office really oval?) I'd always pictured the White House as tall as a skyscraper, with black iron gates all around, and white, frilly curtains in each window that were probably handmade by the First Lady. Yes, indeed. Martin Luther King would have fit quite comfortably.

Who else?

I could also have imagined someone like George Washington Carver being president, just because he was so brilliant and all (and we'd just finished studying him in school). I could visualize him building his own lab down in the White House basement so he could do his experiments any time he wanted. Sure, he'd probably fly all over the world doing important things and helping the sick, poor, and suffering people—but he would probably have a *huge* plot of land out back where he could grow as many peanuts as he'd like, and he could even experiment on them in his secret lab in the White House basement.

I could have imagined *Daddy* as president in a red-hot minute, too. He'd be fair and kind to everybody, and the first two things he would have done as president would be to stop all the wars around the world, then tear down that horrid department store that wouldn't sell his beautiful wife the hat she'd wanted so badly for church. The only really elaborate thing he'd probably request is for somebody to dig him a big fishing hole out back (but not show-offy big) so he could go fishing whenever he wanted. (Did the White House even have a backyard?)

Another few ideas popped into my mind, too: James Earl

Jones would have been a good president, what with his booming voice and barrel chest and all. His mere presence alone would signal to the world that we were a strong country, and all of our enemies would be frightened. Sidney Poitier might have worked well, too—especially since Mother and all my older sisters worshipped the ground he walked on. (Even though I'd never seen one of his movies all the way through, I loved his diction and his dignity, and the way he set people straight so *handily* whenever they tried to insult him.)

Miss Miriam's question about a lady president had me stumped, though. Then, Eureka! Gadzooks! I had it! How about Shirley Temple? I remember hearing my parents talking about the fact that she was even thinking about running for Congress that following year—so that qualified her as a politician, didn't it? Plus, she'd probably invite children from all over the country to the White House, to come and see her great movies, like *Little Princess. Curly Top. Bright Eyes.* Maybe she'd have something like a lottery, where every kid in America got to pick a number, and if their number was selected, they got to fly to Washington, DC, and watch *Heidi* and maybe pop popcorn with President Shirley Temple herself. Pretty cool stuff.

∽

My "political" predictions, all those many years ago, were laughable. Sophomoric and silly-sounding. But they were also based on something tangible and touchable; they were based on hope, faith, and the promise of a bright new future.

These were the powerful beliefs that Miss Miriam had instilled in my little hopeful heart—the promise that we, as a nation (particularly women), were moving into uncharted territory, facing a world filled with promise and possibility. A world with no limits.

And as I stood with Miss Miriam that afternoon, fingering all of her finery, who knew that there'd actually come a day when this little pig-tailed, skinny-legged girl would work in the White House and sit in the Oval Office with the president of the United States? (And yes, the Oval Office is, indeed, oval—but considerably smaller than it appears on television.) Who knew that this little potato-kneed girl from Motown would one day walk her own son through the Rose Garden or speed through the city in the president's motorcade, or introduce him to Mother and Daddy before they left this earthly world? It seemed like a fantastic, faraway fantasy—an Alice-through-the-looking-glass dream—that yes, one day, this little pigtail-wearing girl would walk proudly through the *front entrance* of the West Wing, where black people were at one time expressly forbidden, and yes, she'd live to see the historic day when a black man would be elected to the highest office in the land. *Who knew?*

Miss Miriam did.

Miss Miriam and God.

ᘓᘐ

EVEN through my daydreaming about George Washington Carver and Shirley Temple being in the White House, I could still hear Miss Miriam going on and on about how much progress black people and women have made. Boy, was she revved up!

I didn't quite understand why she was suddenly launching into all this talk about the power of women, but I certainly liked the way it sounded. I was feeling proud about my gender. I AM WOMAN! A proud, independent, forward-thinking *woman*! Why, one day soon, I'd be able to bring home the bacon and burp the baby *at the same time*! And maybe one day, I'd even be brave enough to burn my bra (once I started *wearing* one, that is . . . but let's not put the cart before the horse).

At least not just yet.

For now, mastering the art of walking in high heels was enough of a task.

She reached over and took my hand.

"You are absolutely beautiful, little friend of mine. Don't you ever, *ever* let anyone tell you any different."

I blushed at the compliment. Sometimes I didn't feel beautiful at all. I was, at times, ashamed of the color of my skin and my flyaway, frizzy hair. Virtually all magazine and television ads I ever saw pictured sultry, flaxen-haired,

red-lipped women with tiny waists and creamy, milky-white complexions. Although I was aware on a cognizant, intellectual level, that there was certainly more to the world than pale complexions (heck, my own mother had been a *model*, for pete's sake!), Miss Miriam's compliment that afternoon stirred my pride and bolstered my self-esteem. I also said a silent prayer of gratitude for magazines like *Ebony* and *Jet*, because they lifted me out of my insular little seven-year-old world on the East Side of Detroit and showed me an exciting, sophisticated outside world filled with black people who were smart, savvy, wise, and worldly.

As long as Miss Miriam was in a generous mood with her compliments, I took the chance of hoping she'd be equally as generous with the magical things hanging in her wardrobe. After all, we *were* on the topic of beauty.

"Can we look at some of your gowns?" I asked tentatively, hopefully.

Even the thought of it seemed to infuse her with more energy. Her spirit sat up straighter, right along with her spine. The pull of—and pride in—her glory days of yesteryear seemed to expand the very walls around us. Before I knew it, she was opening doors again, pulling things out. My ears were hungry for the sound of the *swish, swish, swish* of her sequined finery being pulled from the closet.

"Here's one of your favorites," she said in a whisper, as if it were a big surprise.

She was right.

I loved looking at the long lavender gown. The sound of its movement was as powerful and evocative to me as the sight of its beads and bodice. The sleeves were long and tapered, with tiny clusters of pearls around the neckline. I must have gasped. It didn't even smell like mothballs. Nothing in Miss Miriam's house did. Mothballs were definitely not her style.

The only thing her house smelled like was lilac, lavender, talcum powder, and the tiniest hint of Murphy's Oil soap—but all in just the right doses, nothing overpowering the other.

"What say we get this thing on you?" she asked, scanning her neat column of shoe boxes to select the perfect pair—no digging around in a messy closet, desperately trying to find a stray shoe for Miss Miriam, no way in the world. After a moment, she found the right box, expertly yanked it out, then opened the lid to reveal the most beautiful pair of lavender pumps I'd ever seen. I was running out of breath. *Try it on?* Sure, during other visits I'd seen the dress lying across her bed, and I'd always admired it from afar, but trying it on? What if I popped a pearl or busted a bead?

She glanced over at my expression.

"Stop looking so worried, child! Be happy! Be excited! Get ready to get glamorous!" she entreated. "Every woman should know how to move *correctly* in a full-length gown.

You have to know how to move just so to make these beads catch the light in exactly the way you want them to, and you need to know how to make your dress *sound* when you walk! You know . . . that swishing sound I know you love."

My butterflies began their dance.

"You sure about this, Miss Miriam? This gown's way too long for me, and I'm only just getting the hang of the high heels. Maybe I should wait until I'm a little older. I don't want to snag or rip anything."

She actually smirked, maybe in disappointment or mild disgust at my lack of enthusiasm, that I would actually say something so utterly stupid.

"A true lady doesn't wait until the day of the ball to teach herself to move elegantly in her gown," she said crisply, pulling tight the sash around her velvet robe. I think she might have been a little frustrated. "I'll pin it up, of course . . . I don't want you breaking your neck and having your father come down here looking to break *my* neck because I hurt his baby girl! Now get behind that dressing screen, take off those *dungarees* that you're wearing—or whatever you call them—and get into that gown before I change my mind."

The butterflies danced away, floating up into the darkened clouds outside. I was excited, on my way to being Dorothy again—a Dorothy Dandridge with fuzzy pigtails and a beanpole-skinny body. I disappeared behind her Oriental dressing screen, untied my Keds again, and pulled off my T-shirt, careful not to knock over any of her precious things. Even the sudden thunderclap didn't rattle me in the least. I was a little lady on a mission. I was getting ready to get beautiful.

"Wrap that purple silk dressing gown around you—the one that's hanging on the back of that chair—and come on out, for heaven's sake. It's not like you've got that much to hide," she chided me gently. She was excited about the impending fashion show, too. I could tell by her voice.

She was right, again. I didn't have much to wrap, conceal, or cover. My chest was nonexistent ("headlights," one of my aunts called them), and my waist hadn't even developed *into* a waist yet, and I certainly had no hips or backside to speak of at all. Maybe Sheila had been right. Even though we'd made up and become friends again, her description of me as "a skinny-legged beanpole" might have been right on target. But at that same moment—as my self-confidence was beginning to buckle—God nestled Himself straight into my seven-year-old soul: I might be a beanpole—but I bet your bottom dollar that I was about to become the most *elegant* seven-year-old beanpole *this* Motor City had ever seen.

Shyly, slowly, I emerged from behind the dressing screen. Miss Miriam had already retrieved her pincushion (the one shaped like a strawberry), ready to adjust the hem and the sleeves. Her spine-straight posture was another indication to me that she was as excited as all get-out. I listened carefully to her instructions:

"Now when I put this over your head, don't move a muscle. Just hold your head up straight and your arms up in the air even straighter, pointing toward the ceiling. When I tell you to, slip your right arm through the right sleeve, then your left arm through the left, okay?"

It was getting complicated—all these instructions—and I didn't want to mess it up. I did as I was instructed, standing ramrod straight until I was told otherwise.

And then the magic came.

The sound and feel of the thousands of tiny beads showered around my head and shoulders, cool on my skin. But I dared not move a muscle until I heard from Miss Miriam, the boss.

"Good girl," she said, mumbling now through the straight pins pursed between her lips. "Now slowly lift up your head and slip your right arm through. Good. Now your left. Now let me get these old knees of mine working, so that I can kneel down and get you all hemmed up," she mumbled through the pins, leaning over as nimble as a gymnast. "Stay still, girl!"

After a moment or two of her leaning down toward the bottom of the gown, busy putting straight pins into the hem, we were ready.

"Head up high," she said crisply, this First Lady of Fashion.

My head snapped up to full attention. I even had the nerve to lift my chin again ever so slightly. I wasn't even Dorothy now. I was *Nefertiti*. I was a beautiful black swan. My neck felt two feet long, and if I'd had feathers, I would have preened them right then and there. I stood gamely on my tiptoes, trying to gain the height required to be womanly. Quick as a flash, Miss Miriam slipped first my right foot then my left into her matching, magical lavender pumps. *Keds, be gone! Thank you, again, God and Jesus, for this precious, gown-giving woman who's teaching me how to walk in heels. Bring on the thunder, and I will not be scared. I'll even confront those sharp-toothed monsters that live underneath our basement stairs the minute I get home! I am woman! I am brave! And I look good, too!*

Miss Miriam sat up straight, regarding me fully and with a great degree of pride, then issued her command: "Now *walk*, little woman, *walk!*"

Obediently and instinctively, I walked gingerly across the room. My poor toes were jammed together like sardines, but that's just the price you have to pay for wearing a pretty pump. And then, I did it: *I squeezed the inside of my toes—and it worked!*

Miss Miriam sat at the edge of the bed, legs crossed, pincushion in her lap. She was clapping in tiny, quiet, seal-like claps, giddy as a schoolgirl. "Strut your stuff, child! Make it yours!"

I was on the verge of feeling confused and a little disoriented because of all the directions, instructions, and commands she was yelling, but I kept up with her. I did as I was told.

I walked, in her beaded gown and high-heeled shoes, from one end of the room to the other. I even had the nerve to sway my nonexistent hips the tiniest little bit, like I'd seen Lena Horne sway in her movies. Oh buddy, did I walk. Back and forth across her bedroom. I walked.

Without stumbling.

"Slow down when you walk. You're too pretty to rush. *Let them wait!* Negro women have been rushed and herded and pushed this way and that for far too long. It's *our* time now, Chipper! Take tiny steps. You're not playing Mother-May-I, for Lord's sake, so why are you taking such giant steps? No, baby doll, you're strutting at the Savoy now. So make it count."

A full-length mirror stood in one corner of the room. It must have been God himself who led my steps toward that mirror without wobbling. I looked. *Thank you again, God. I actually do look like a Savoy lady! Thank you for Miss Miriam. Thank you for her beauty and elegance.*

I tiny-stepped my way back toward Miss Miriam and ended up collapsing into her waiting arms. Even in the beaded gown and heels, our embrace was urgent. I hoped and prayed that none of the beads had fallen off while we were hugging, but I didn't really care about that. I was in her arms.

Just that quickly, I surrendered to the sweet pull of my imagination, so I stood up again. I was the most famous actress in the world, preparing for one final sashay down the red carpet. I could even hear the muted, popping sounds of the photographer's lightbulbs flashing, and the drowned-out screams of my adoring fans. I could feel the crush of reporters as they pushed themselves against the wood barriers, shouting out questions about my newest love interest and my upcoming movie. Random pieces of paper were being thrust into my hands—*those pesky autograph seekers*! I turned again toward the mirror.

"Now give me a pivot, baby! *Pivot!*"

My first thought was, *What in heaven's name is a "pivot"? A fancy ballroom dance that adults do?* I'd heard Mother and Daddy talk about the Lindy Hop and the fox-trot, but never ever the pivot. I didn't want to disappoint her, so I stood there, waiting. It was the first time I'd ever heard the word— and every time I hear the word spoken (even today, as an adult) my mind hearkens back to the miraculous Miss Miriam.

In the twinkling of an eye, all the reporters and flash-bulbs and screaming fans vaporized into thin air. I was Kristin again—the little girl who didn't even know what the word *pivot* meant.

Miss Miriam saved my hide without even recognizing it.

"*Turn*, baby! Let me see you turn!"

So that's what "pivot" means? To turn?

Still, I vowed to ask Mother to help me look it up in our dog-eared Webster's Dictionary as soon as I got home. I wanted to read the literal definition for myself. (Plus, it pleased Mother to no end when I asked her to help me look up certain words in the dictionary.)

But back to the task at hand, which was considerable: Miss Miriam was asking me to "pivot" in high-heeled shoes *and* a full-length gown that was twice the length of my body! Had she lost her ever-loving mind?

It was at that point that I figured if I was ever going to be a lady's lady, if I was ever going to embrace grace and wrap confidence around my shoulders, now was as good a time to begin as any. So I turned slowly, toes squeezed tight, beaded arms stretched out long and luxuriously at each side.

Miss Miriam clapped again, then put one hand to her mouth. It looked, for a frightening minute, like she was going to cry, but then she smiled a bright smile, opened her arms, and I walked over to her, collapsing into her embrace again. It was time to take off the dress and shoes.

My feet hurt.

As I was changing behind the screen, I could hear Miss Miriam moving around the room, picking up things and straightening up. By the time I'd laced my Keds and emerged from behind the dressing screen, her bedroom was back in order: the pincushion put away, the gown hung up, and the shoes returned to their proper box.

She was on bended knee again, though—this time, carefully sifting through a steamer trunk filled with beautiful, ladylike things. I remember thinking that it very well might have been a magical trunk, packed full of the items that helped make ladies become even more beautiful than they already were. Without turning around, she extended her right arm backward toward me.

"You might as well take this little number for yourself, because *I'm* not going to be using it anytime soon. Lord knows I've had my share of fun in my younger days, but now it's time to pass that mantle on to someone else."

I didn't even want to look at what was in her hands. I was concerned about her voice. She *really* sounded like there were tears in it now. Plus, she refused to turn around and look at me. She just kept her head bent down toward the contents in the steamer trunk. This wasn't good. Old people weren't supposed to get sad; it didn't seem fair. Eventually, I gazed down at the object in her hand: a beaded evening bag, with strings of tinier beads hanging down from the bottom. It was fairly heavy in my hands, too, and the inside was lined with ivory satin.

The hairs at the nape of my neck were beginning to rise. Hot tears began to pool. My breathing suddenly felt shallow, as if someone were pinching my nose closed. I just couldn't get enough oxygen into my little lungs. The pure power of love was moving through every corner of that room. Its magnetic intensity threatened to carry me away. But her words helped calm me down.

"Take good care of that thing, child. I've had that bag for eons."

And then she paused. "Something tells me," she said very slowly, all quiet and reflective now, "that my dress-up days are over . . . but yours have not yet even begun."

I knew, then, that her heart was full and her mind was dancing with memories of yesterdays long, long ago. Her voice caught as she spoke. I was beginning to feel bad. I didn't come to visit to make her cry. *Good Lord.*

She refused to move away from that trunk, and her back was still turned toward me, which I thought was rather odd. So I knelt beside her and hugged her from behind. Miss Miriam was my heroine and my friend. Even Sheila wouldn't believe that Miss Miriam's fancy-shmancy evening bag was now mine; she wouldn't believe me even if I swore on the grave of my now-dead goldfish, Chomper. I could barely believe it myself.

But in that same moment, I realized something else: Miss Miriam's steamer trunk held, for her, not only precious baubles, but pleasing memories of her past.

It was her own version of a Forever Box.

I felt bountifully blessed that she'd chosen little old *me* to help preserve such a precious part of her past, and I had every intention of taking my newfound role as memory-maker very, very seriously. These women—these wonderful, wizened women who were my friends—were entrusting me with invaluable, irreplaceable pieces of their past, and even then, I recognized the magnitude of their acts.

Even though they fully recognized—and fully embraced—their own finite mortality, they still wanted me to pass parts of themselves along to future generations. They expected me to carry a tiny piece of their existence with me into the future. And they were entrusting me to cherish their stories, and to chase away all the cobwebs that threatened to obscure their memories.

And then, before I knew it, Miss Miriam had moved back over to her vanity table. The woman was nimble and quick, I'll tell you that much. She scanned the vanity table, touching each of her perfume bottles lightly with her index finger.

She stopped at one, turning toward me.

"I just must be in a giving mood today, child. You caught me on the right day. Now, take this perfume bottle and keep it for yourself. You can even use it right now—spritz some lightly on your wrist before you go home and I bet you dollars to doughnuts your mother will be pleased."

The bottle was white and delicately fluted, with two

colorful butterflies on one side and two lovely tulips on the other. I didn't know what to do.

"Take it!" she whispered urgently. *Well gosh! She's being bossy again, isn't she?*

She said it again, this time with a smile. "You better take this bottle before I change my mind."

Having said those words, I grabbed the bottle (somewhat greedily, I'm sure she probably thought), and thanked her profusely. All of my gift-giving friends were leaving me important parts of themselves, and I felt honored and humbled. They were leaving me things they wanted me to remember them by. And I would cherish each item for the rest of my life, making sure to pass them along to my own children, when I finally had them, so that they, too, could remember Miss Miriam's kind spirit and hear the shared stories.

Miss Miriam had turned thoughtful, sentimental even, and, unfortunately, a little wistful.

"Now when you grow up and wear long gowns, you'll know how to move. What to do. The proper way to walk. Don't ever forget it, my sweet. And if you ever have children—and I pray that you will—teach them grace and humility. Teach your daughters how to walk in long gowns and high heels, smiling all the time—even if their feet are hurting so badly their toes are singing Dixie. Teach them how to smile *into* themselves—that way, when they're at a fancy party, their smile won't be fake or forced because it'll be coming from some very real place deep, down inside their own souls. Don't forget that."

I was a little confused. How can someone "smile into themselves"? And who in the world smiles when they don't really want to? (How innocently naive I was back then. Little did I know that, in today's rough-and-tumble world, *fake* smiles are almost as common as the real ones.)

She continued, tossing out advice left and right: "Rely on your own natural beauty. Don't get me wrong, now: There's nothing wrong with enhancing your beauty—but don't let those enhancements *define* you. Be subtle in everything. When you start wearing lipstick, don't slap it on like you're painting Mr. Sexton's picket fence. Apply it lightly, so people can barely tell you have any on."

Miss Miriam was actually crying now; quiet tears that just about broke my little heart. (I hate to say it, but it's the truth: Lots of people look downright ugly when they cry. But not Miss Miriam. Even her tears were graceful.)

The conversation had shifted slightly. I could tell she was not only talking about simple fashion tips, but about life in general—about what's right and wrong.

"When you grow up, sweetie, *always* remember to treat others with kindness and respect. Even when you're dressed to the nines and all decked out in your Sunday best, remember to treat people with dignity and decorum. Never get too big for your britches. God doesn't like that at all."

She scoffed slightly, wrinkling her nose.

"I've seen these movie stars on TV so taken with themselves that they forget about the other people around them," she said with what sounded to me like disgust.

"I don't care *what* color your skin is—black or white or purple with red polka dots—*all women* should behave with an eye toward kindness, compassion, and universal love. Believe me when I tell you that it doesn't take beads or bangles to make a person pretty—it takes a generous spirit and a gracious disposition."

She was getting louder again. She pointed her finger at me.

"You're as pretty as a picture, Chipper—but never *ever* become so preoccupied with your own beauty that you blind yourself to the people around you. That right there is downright ugly behavior. And, as you've probably already heard, God don't like ugly."

She was on a roll.

"If a woman is pretty on the outside and mean or cruel on the inside, then she's as ugly as a mile of unpaved road. Here are the things you should always remember, particularly as it relates to your growing into a proper young lady: Always be kind to others. Work *hard* to stay pretty—on the inside and well-presented on the outside. When you're speaking with someone, look them straight in the eye. If they say something funny, don't hee-haw like an ol' mule;

instead, smile and laugh a light, graceful laugh. Be humble
in all things—never brash or arrogant or wild-acting. And
remember: Satin pumps don't make the woman; it's the *inner
beauty of the woman who makes the satin pumps!*"

She really tickled herself with that last line, because she
laughed out loud—a soft, tinkling laugh that sounded like
my grandmother's crystal. As for me, I was just glad she'd
stopped crying.

I was pretty sure I knew what she was saying, but I hadn't
been able to absorb absolutely *everything*. (What did "preoccupied" and "brash" mean again?) All in all, though, I knew
she was telling me to always be nice, even if I grew up to be
a fancy lady who wore beaded gowns.

She was winding down. She had to have been a little
tired, I thought as I watched her straightening the combs
and perfume bottles on her vanity. Miss Miriam was ready
to rest.

I leaned over and kissed her on her cheek.

"Good-bye, Miss Miriam. Please don't go out in all this
rain. If you need something, you *know* my mom will send
one of us girls over right away. Just call and one of us will
come a-running. I love the bag and the perfume you gave
me, and I promise to remember what you said about beauty
and being nice and about how great women are. I can't see
myself having children any time soon, 'cause I'm still just a
kid myself—but if I do, I promise to share these beautiful

items with them one day. I love you so, so much. Now get some rest. I'll be back to visit in a couple of days."

After I left her bedroom, I hightailed it down the steps— a wide staircase in the middle of the foyer, if I remember correctly—and sprinted into her kitchen. No longer were the little monsters lurking in the shadows. I sauntered into the room bravely, swaggering like John Wayne in the Wild West.

There was the drawer: a deep, metal bread drawer with a fairly heavy lid. Pulling it open, I grabbed two pinwheel cookies and sat down at her kitchen table to eat them. I didn't like the sliced pecans on top, but I ate them anyway because I didn't want to hurt her feelings.

I was careful not to leave even a crumb behind. When I was finished, I rose from the table and strode with confidence over to the kitchen phone on the wall to call Mother so she could meet me across the street. I wondered, briefly, what Miss Miriam was doing right at that moment, upstairs alone in her bedroom—but most of all I thought about how lucky I was to have a woman like her in my life. At the bottom of the stairs, I yelled up (without *screaming*, mind you): "I'm leaving now, Miss Miriam, but I'll be back in a few days! Thank you again—so very, very much—for the purse and the perfume! I promise to keep them forever!"

"Okay, sweetie pie! You're my little lady now! Take good care of that bottle I gave you! The perfume is from Europe!"

And then, as if in afterthought, she yelled downstairs again.

"You eat your cookies?" (By then, I could tell she was growing weary of all the yelling back and forth; Lord knows that hollering through her house was definitely not something she did on a regular basis. Tacky and undignified to the extreme.)

"Yes, ma'am. I had two cookies, and they were delicious! Thank you! I love you! I love you! Good-bye!"

"Good-bye, my sweet! I love you, too! Come again and I'll teach you the fox-trot!"

Outside, Mother stood waiting patiently with her black umbrella. Looking both ways, I ran across the street and sought comfort and cover under our wide, safe umbrella; our shield. I showed her the perfume and the purse, and she smiled quietly.

"That Miss Miriam is something else indeed," Mother said with a hint of awe in her voice. "You're lucky to have her as such a good friend."

And then Mother leaned down closer, sniffing the air around me. I smiled, embarrassed.

"You certainly smell good, Beauty!"

I smiled as close to a grown-up smile as I could muster. Pride swam all around my little head like hot air.

"Why thank you, kind miss!" I answered, curtsying in my rain boots.

Mother continued with our jesting. "You absolutely *must* give me the name of your perfume, ma'am," she said, gazing down at me with a knowing smile.

"Of course, of course," I answered back, trying my level best to sound like a haughty, nose-turned-up-in-the-air fancy lady. "I'll even let you spray some on your wrist if you like . . . but just a little bit, if you don't mind. It's from Europe, and it's very, very precious." *Where was Europe again?*

We continued walking toward home, avoiding the puddles, feeling solid and safe under Daddy's big umbrella.

As we walked, I scrunched my toes up real hard inside my Keds so I could be *just a little* more elegant. When we finally got to our house, my feet hurt so bad they were barking like Chihuahuas. But I had my gifts from Miss Miriam.

When we got to the top of the porch, Mother shook the raindrops off the umbrella, closed it up tightly, then leaned down and spoke to me directly, face to face:

"Take good care of your things. You might want to use them later," she said simply.

She opened our screen door and we walked into the house together. Inside, after I'd kicked off my Keds and rain boots, I bounded upstairs, heading straight to the linen closet in the hallway. I reached in and yanked out a fresh towel, then retreated to the bathroom and locked the door behind me. Carefully, slowly, I wrapped both the purse and the perfume in the towel. Even through the thick towel, I could smell the fragrance of Miss Miriam's fancy European perfume.

Next, I snuck into Mother and Daddy's bedroom and riffled through their closet until I found what I was looking for.

Even though my feet still hurt like the dickens, I carefully placed one foot—then the other—into a pair of Mother's favorite leather pumps. And for the next few minutes, I was transformed again . . . into a glorious, grown-up fancy lady who knew how to walk in shimmering, satin pumps simply by squeezing the insides of her toes.

I felt strong now—invincible. Fearless. Newly matured, and mightily empowered, thanks to my friendship with Miss Miriam.

Pumped up and full of bravado, I began to feel boisterous. It was time to take another big step—literally and figuratively. Approaching the basement door, I yanked it open, peered down the long, dark staircase, then actually took two or three steps down. It was the first time I'd ventured down into our basement alone. But this was something I *had* to do, a mission I just *had* to accomplish. When I got to the bottom, without hesitating, I snuck a peek underneath the stairs, fully prepared to confront those pesky little sharp-toothed monsters face to face. They just didn't scare me anymore. I looked underneath the stairs again. Nothing. Only a few cardboard boxes and my rusted-out tricycle. (I'd *long* since graduated to my two-wheeled banana bike . . . tricycles were for babies.) Those mangy monsters had lost their power!

I ran back up, taking the stairs two at a time. I was proud and puffed up. I felt so in control. And even more than that, I was *finally* free of fear.

∾

TODAY, whenever I entertain guests or attend elaborate events, Miss Miriam is the person who most immediately comes to my mind. Even as I'm rushing about in excited preparation—most often, dashing from closet to bedroom to bathroom—I hear her words of wisdom: "Slow down. Don't rush. Let them wait!" Her words calm my spirit and soothe my soul.

Miss Miriam was a woman's woman; her every movement and memory epitomized grace, elegance . . . and, most of all, humility. When she passed away, part of her life continued through me. How? Because today, my own adult daughter walks with grace and elegance, but humility is what showers over her soul. Today, I know, as does my own daughter, that physical beauty is fleeting—and that real beauty emerges from the inside out. We both know how important it is to recognize that no amount of makeup, bedazzling jewelry, or even worldwide fame can make a cruel person beautiful.

What defines true beauty?

A kind and compassionate spirit.

Dignified, respectful behavior.

Spiritual generosity, and the enhanced ability to empathize with others.

Today, Miss Miriam's memory still burns on within my spirit—and my goal is to impart her wisdom upon all women who are trying hard to embrace their own intelligence, inherent power, and inner beauty. Miss Miriam's words of wisdom were simple, straightforward, and startlingly honest. This is what she taught me, and this is what I pass along now:

1. Constantly remind yourself of the fact that you are your own unique definition of beautiful—whatever that definition means to you.

2. If you have children (not necessarily your own biological children, but *any* youth in your life), teach them—through your own actions—that *true beauty is an inside job.*

3. Go about your daily duties with grace and confidence.

4. No matter how pretty or powerful you are, you must *always treat others with respect.* Haughtiness is unattractive—not to mention sinful—and the *only* time it's ever acceptable to look down on someone is if you're getting

ready to pick them *up*. So whether you're walking the red carpet on your way to your own movie premiere, or walking down the alley, kicking an old, rusty coffee can, treat others as you would want them to treat you. Whether you're air-kissing others at a fancy White House soiree, or pitching horseshoes at a family reunion in the public park, never *ever* stick your nose too far up in the air—because it just might get *stuck up there*, and then where on earth would you be?

5. And as old-fashioned as this may sound, always try to look your best. Take care of yourself, mentally, physically, and spiritually. Don't look sloppy.

Today, my beaded evening bag and fluted perfume bottle are tucked away in my Forever Box. I bring them out often, to transport myself back to that magical afternoon in Miss Miriam's bedroom, where I first learned to walk in high heels and where I learned how to *swish* when I walked. It is the memory of Miss Miriam, and

other women like her, who remind me to love and respect everyone equally—and to celebrate the inherent beauty of all women, everywhere.

Physical beauty is elusive and mercurial.

Genuine beauty comes from within.

And remember this: A sequined gown doesn't make the woman . . . it's the inner beauty of a woman that makes the sequined gown!

Mary Elizabeth Sorsby
COURTESY OF THE AUTHOR

VICTORIOUS

---❧---

I AWOKE THE NEXT morning with a smile in my heart, even though the sky was still smoldering gray. Thunderclouds rolled and roiled in the far distance. Those old clouds did nothing to dampen my enthusiasm, though—because today was the day that belonged to sweet Mama Lilly, my maternal grandmother. Today was the day she would pull me gently to her soft, talcum-powdery bosom and whisper how much she loved me, the youngest grandchild of my mother's seven children. Today was the day Daddy would toss both me and my red plaid overnight bag into the backseat of our station wagon and drive me to her neat little low-lying house on the other side of the city, so that I could actually spend the night with this softly plump, pillowy woman. Such an excursion was, to me anyway, a bright, bold adventure. My excitement knew no bounds. As I nibbled on buttered toast (Wonder Bread, my favorite) and Cream of Wheat for breakfast in the final minutes before our departure, I could barely even breathe.

Good-bye, kitchen chair, I whispered to myself as I rose from the table to carry my dishes to the sink. *I'm so, so sorry you won't be able to come and join me in my adventure.* Almost pulsating with excitement, I plunged my thin brown arms up to my elbows in warm soapy water, scrubbing my Cream of Wheat bowl vigorously. Searching for the dish towel so that I could dry my dishes and place them back in our cupboard, my gaze fell upon our white enamel teapot, sitting, as usual, at the left rear burner of our stove. I actually regarded it with something close to pity, simply because it had to remain stationary in its same old boring place on the stove. No, it wouldn't be joining me on my excellent adventure to Mama Lilly's. I bid it adieu. *Farewell, kitchen teapot. Shine on brightly— and keep boiling your fine, fresh water without me while I'm away.* The remainder of the morning passed much the same way until I heard Daddy yell from upstairs, "You all ready, Buttercup? It's time to shake a leg! Kiss everybody good-bye and let's get on the road! I want to beat the traffic."

His words were music to my ears.

Fare thee well, clear windowpane, I said, rapping gently on the delicate glass of our front hall window as I prepared to leave.

Until tomorrow, metal mailbox, I whispered as we walked out onto the front porch and lifted its hinged lid one last time, letting it fall back into place with an unceremonious clap.

Daddy and I made our move.

Now fully outside and truly, unmistakably, *officially* on our way, we walked hand in hand to the car. Coming to the edge of our freshly mowed front lawn, I knelt quickly and plucked a few blades of grass, clasping them neatly in the palm of my small brown fist. These blades of grass were the lucky ones. I opened my fist and smiled. *As for you, tender green blades of grass, you get to come with me!*

Right then, Daddy's strong arms swung my body high up into the air, bringing me down in a wide, smooth arch, and nestling me gently into the backseat. I clasped the grass tightly, tucking the freshly pulled blades into the front pocket of my overnight bag. Never mind the fact that, in plucking the grass, I'd also pulled a great glob of mud from the still-moist earth as well. Who cared? What could one expect after three full days of rain? Yes, it would create a mess, but Mother would surely launder everything as soon as I returned home. I pictured her standing in front of our washing machine in the basement, pulling the mud-stained clothes out of my overnight bag and maybe smiling to herself as she separated the soiled items. *What am I going to do with my Beauty?* she'd think, shaking her head in quiet admiration as she sprinkled in a cupful of Tide. *My baby girl is always trying to pluck and save every little thing in her path to create memories for later. Even blades of grass.*

My father leaned forward in the front seat and turned the key in the ignition. After a few false starts, our station wagon roared to life. Daddy checked his rearview mirror, smiling at me as he backed up. I caught his wink in the mirror—a wink and a smile, directed only toward me! (He was also a wonderful winker, by the way.)

I was in heaven.

Before I knew it, we had arrived.

Hand in hand again, Daddy and I walked up Mama Lilly's front steps together. They were painted a dark, dark green in several thick, shiny coats—to make the porch look more like grass than cement, I guessed.

❦

WITH Daddy gone and me now all alone with Mama Lilly, the ions in the air seemed to change. Every room in her home somehow suddenly felt *emptier*—yet filled to overflowing with adventure and possibility. I didn't want to venture into any room without her—not because I was frightened, but because my sole desire was to be in as close proximity to my grandmother as was physically possible. I wanted and needed to share her same space, to drink in her gentle energy, to allow the molecules of our bodies to commingle and reacquaint themselves all over again, as eagerly as if we were strangers or brand-new friends.

If Mama Lilly moved from the kitchen to the dining room, I followed close behind, her miniaturized shadow. If she wanted to retrieve something from one of the bedrooms— a pillow or a quilt or a shiny trinket to show me—she knew instinctively to wait a minute or two, until I realized she was leaving the room, which gave me time to catch up with her so we could walk *together*, hand in hand.

For some strange reason, the sun *always* seemed to be shining in Mama Lilly's sparkling kitchen. I could never quite figure that out. Even at *night*, the room seemed to brighten, an otherworldly glow. Not a scary, alien-from-another-planet, radioactive glow, but rather, a warmth so powerful it filled the room with spiritual light and love. It sounds hokey, I know, but it's the truth: Not once in my little life had I *ever* been scared to move around in her kitchen. Not even at night. Not even in the dark—and you *know* how I am about the dark.

In her kitchen, every appliance shone as brightly as the North Star. Her refrigerator, a bulky Frigidaire the size of a boat, hummed quietly in a corner beside the screen door. On her kitchen table were a green-and-white-striped napkin holder and a clear bottle of what I always called "zacarin," a clear liquid used for sweetening tea and coffee.

Just inside her pantry, she kept a metal stepstool. I'd

always been impressed with how that stepstool was designed: when it wasn't being used, it stood flat against the pantry wall. But when you needed to use it, you simply pulled a little latch on the side and three stair steps magically unfolded, forming a miniature ladder. Quite clever.

There we stood in her sparkling kitchen, rays of sunshine ricocheting off the chrome appliances, the sheer curtains stirring lightly in the breeze. Instinctively, I knew that it was time for her to decide what to make for our dinner. My soul smiled in laughter and in love.

I watched as she opened the heavy-as-a-load-of-bricks refrigerator door and leaned in, her eyebrows furrowed in measured concentration. I prayed a silent prayer: *Pleasepleaseplease, Lord, let it be fried chicken. Please let her pull out chicken from her great, gleaming refrigerator, so I can stand close by and watch as she drops each floured piece into that bubbling, boiling grease—grease so hot it makes you think of heaven and hell at the same time. Fry it up real good, Mama Lilly, till every piece is golden brown and my mouth is watering like a little outdoor spigot.*

And always, she'd enlist my help.

Even before the frying began, I knew exactly what to do—because we'd done it so many times before. I'd drag that wonderful, expandable stepstool over to her cupboard so that I could scramble up to the third shelf, where she kept the spices. Sure as shooting, there I'd find the navy blue cylindrical container—the one that pictured the Umbrella

Girl, spilling salt as she walked in the rain, covered by her oversized umbrella. I'd hand the container down to my grandmother ever so carefully and sometimes, if she was in the right mood, she'd even allow me to shake the Morton salt directly onto the chicken as she was frying it up.

Ours was a carefully choreographed concert. Our kitchen dance was all our own. And on that one special afternoon, after I'd shaken the salt and unfolded the TV tables, we settled ourselves in front of her living room television. (Her TV, a behemoth floor-model RCA that seemed to take up half the room, sported a wire coat hanger on its top—"for clearer reception," according to my grandmother, who'd promptly removed the rabbit-ear antennae as soon as the TV had arrived from the store.)

Positioning ourselves close to each other but a few feet away from the TV, we'd eat an early chicken dinner while watching *Bonanza.*

"I do love that handsome Ben Cartwright," she sighed as the opening credits came onto the screen.

My seven-year-old memory of Mama Lilly, at least as it related to her beloved *Bonanza,* was that she admired the widowed Ben Cartwright and his three caring, capable sons, Adam, Hoss, and Little Joe. She loved the otherworldly allure of the Cartwright's lush and lovely thousand-acre Ponderosa Ranch—so starkly different from the densely packed neighborhoods of inner-city Detroit where we lived.

That was precisely what I loved most about Mama Lilly—the deliberate, almost dutiful manner in which she transported herself from her beautiful little tidy house in the city to a larger, infinitely more exciting world of foreign interests and borderless boundaries. Yes, she loved her life, her church, and her family with a pure and powerful force—but she also loved the larger, looming universe around her and, unlike many elderly women, she didn't shirk from it at all. She forced herself to explore different worlds; places that would have, under normal circumstances, been strictly off-limits to elderly black women in the mid 1960s.

She'd recently returned from an expedition to Egypt, and she'd come back all revved up about the history of our culture. Even then, I knew it was rare for a woman—black *or* white—to travel so far, especially at such an advanced age. She'd absorbed so much on that particular trip, and she couldn't wait to share her experience with me.

"Traveling to Egypt reminded me all over again that our people are strong and resilient, Krissy Baby. You *do* know that the dawn of civilized society began in Africa, don't you, sweetheart?"

I watched her watching me. She looked so *proud*.

"Our African forefathers created sophisticated societies, developed commerce and trade, and led the rest of the world into the Age of Enlightenment."

I visualized my grandmother's plane landing in Egypt,

rolling right up to the door of a famous pyramid or something. I could just see her, slowly disembarking after the long flight, taking her sweet time stepping down onto the tarmac. Maybe she wiped her forehead with the embroidered handkerchief she always kept close. Very quickly, probably, she adapted to the rhythm of the country and the Continent, making that rhythm all her own. I imagined her purposefully placing her dainty little feet onto the very soil from which her own, not-too-distant forefathers sprang.

Yes, indeed, Mama Lilly was a woman who remained active and vitally engaged until the very end of her life. Staying in only one place and doing only one thing didn't interest her at all. And on this day, she was certainly excited about Egypt.

"Cairo was definitely my favorite spot," she confided.

Immediately, my mind painted a picture of my beautiful, silver-haired grandmother negotiating the busy back streets of Cairo, maybe riding on a donkey cart through a crowded bazaar, or careening through the crowded city streets in a beat-up taxicab. In the distance, she could probably see those stately white mosques or maybe even some more pyramids. (My geography skills weren't exactly great, so I wasn't even sure if the pyramids were anywhere *near* the city of Cairo. But it was a wonderful image, so I decided that they were.)

"What was special about Cairo?" I asked. I really wanted to know.

"For one, it's a city filled with wonderment and honor," she said in a voice filled with respect. Her eyes took on a faraway look.

Wonderment and honor? Who actually used words like that in normal conversation? She was definitely my Mother's mother. Both of them spoke the King's English at all times— even when they were conversing with seven-year-olds like me.

She continued with her list.

"Secondly, I just love the history behind the actual name of the city—'Cairo'—because I've heard it means 'victorious' in Arabic. Did you know that, honey? Well, it's the truth . . . and Lord knows, we are a 'victorious' people, aren't we, baby?"

At that moment, I promised myself to name our next family pet Cairo—whether it was another cat, dog, or even a goldfish. I liked the sound of the word *victorious* (even if I hadn't been completely sure of its definition). To me, the word sounded *strong*, like an army of a thousand men, all riding Arabian horses, carrying shining silver shields and gleaming swords so sharp they could lob off your ear (or your head) in a single stroke. I decided I liked the word as much as she did—because whenever I was with my miraculous grandmother, I felt *victorious* myself.

I felt safe. *Victoriously safe.*

Suddenly, she snapped her fingers, as if she'd just remembered something pretty important. I was holding my breath.

"Mama brought you something special back from Cairo, baby."

I didn't want to appear greedy or overeager (Mother would certainly have disapproved), but boy, was I curious. What on earth had she brought back for me, all the way from Africa?

"Give me a minute to try to remember where I put it."

I sat quietly in my armchair, hoping and praying that God would enlighten her and guide her toward the gift she'd purchased for me. He must have heard my prayers, because seconds later, she was barking out instructions:

"Run to my bedroom and bring Mama that cardboard box in my closet," she instructed. I could feel my fingers beginning to tingle; I was about to receive a gift from my grandmother! I wanted to laugh and shout or maybe dance a little jig, but I also realized that something about that moment called for a certain solemnity. Some serious sharing was about to occur.

I was so excited, I didn't even have time to be scared about going into her bedroom by myself. I knew there weren't monsters, but one can never be completely certain of such things. Still, I ran like the wind to her bedroom. I didn't want to waste one minute—not only because I was eager to see what she'd brought me, but because it was gradually beginning to dawn on me that, yes, I *would* be alone in the bedroom without her. I didn't like it one bit.

As soon as I entered, I bolted straight to her closet, yanking open her closet door with such force that the doorknob fell off. There on the floor was the box, just like she'd promised. The minute I saw it, I realized that I'd seen it many times before, but had never given it so much as a thought. I regarded it warily. It looked kind of heavy. *Did she expect me to lug that big thing all the way back to the living room by myself?*

I didn't realize it at the time, but that was Mama Lilly's version of her own Forever Box. It was corrugated cardboard, a little beat-up and bent at the corners, but filled with thick, dark fabrics of royal blue velvet, chocolate brown brocade, and satin so dark it looked like midnight. My heart told me that what was *inside* the box was quite special long before my brain did. I realized I was handling history. *Her* history. I think I might have shivered.

She yelled from the living room, "Is it too heavy for you to pick up by yourself, baby? If so, just holler and Mama will come help."

Nothing doing. I wasn't about to make my elderly grandmother haul a heavy box even one step.

I'd do it by myself.

Bending over, I picked up the box by its base, staggering a little underneath its weight. I lurched forward, almost tripping over the fallen doorknob on the floor. If I had actually tripped, all her precious stuff would have come tumbling out, and I would have just died a thousand deaths right then and there. Even at seven, I recognized well the importance of handling precious items with reverence and care.

"I'm coming, Mama Lilly!" I yelled, hoisting the box a bit higher so that the lid came just below my nose. "I'll be there in a quick jiffy!"

In the living room, the ions in the air had changed yet again, becoming super-charged, you might say. Mama Lilly must have felt it too. A thin line of perspiration shone on her top lip, and she smiled an excited smile, reaching for the box.

"Set it right down here, baby," she instructed, and I did as told.

"Now open it carefully and reach in."

Time seemed to slow. Part of me felt like I was being transported to another place. I peeked inside and saw a thick swatch of deep blue velvet the color of royalty. Mama Lilly was leaning in right beside me, pointing down into the box. I held my breath.

"Pull that velvet off the top, very, very carefully," she said.

Using her own two hands, Mama Lilly reached into the box and gently pulled out the package. Turning toward me, she gingerly placed the velvet-covered gift into my hands. I adjusted my little body accordingly so that my lap could create the space I needed to open my present. All of a sudden, everything had become so somber and serious. For goodness' sake—weren't we just humming the opening tune to

Bonanza together, giggling about Hoss's ridiculously large, ten-gallon hat and whispering about how handsome Little Joe was? But I could feel in my heart that something special was about to happen; some magical moment was about to occur between my grandmother and I.

Out of respect for the moment itself, I placed my gift—very carefully, mind you—on the arm of the chair and walked over to the television to turn down the volume. The moment felt like it deserved to be experienced quietly. Mama Lilly liked that I did that. She smiled a soft smile, her eyes dancing as she watched me sit back down.

"Open it, baby! Unwrap that velvet so you can see what's inside. Don't be such a slowpoke. Mama's going to celebrate another birthday just waiting on you!" She was pretty excited.

I pushed away the velvet. Suddenly, I was holding an object I knew had to be mine. It *felt* like it belonged to me—like it had belonged to me maybe even before I was born. Mama Lilly leaned forward, smiling.

"It's for you. I saw it sitting on a rickety old shelf while I was shopping in Cairo. For some reason, I thought of you the minute I saw it, and I knew I had to get it for you."

I peered closer, my heart pounding about five million times a minute.

There it sat. An off-white leather purse, with leather drawstrings. There were gold-embossed drawings on the purse—images of Egypt that, for me, brought the ancient country to life. At the bottom of the purse, a drawing of three gold camels, marching in a line. Just above the camels, an ancient column (like the kind in Rome). There was also a gold-embossed drawing of a tree (which I assumed must be a special Egyptian tree, because I'd never seen one like it growing in Detroit.)

I sat frozen in my chair.

"That's your special purse from Cairo, now," Mama Lilly said. "You take it to church with you or carry it whenever you want to feel special. If you treat it with care, it will last a long, long time."

I touched it very lightly, worried that the oil on my hand from my fried chicken dinner might stain the precious leather. Already, I cherished my Egyptian purse with such fervor I would have slept with it under my pillow had I not been worried about the weight of my head denting it all up. I loved that purse more than fresh strawberries. More than making snow angels in the backyard. Even more than apple butter in the fall or dancing with Daddy in our kitchen.

Mama Lilly gazed over at me, eyes twinkling with love.

"Thank you, Mama Lilly," I whispered, trying mightily not to cry. *What a baby.* "I love my purse, and I'll keep it forever."

She smiled—kind of sadly, I thought.

"Forever's a mighty long time, child. How about just taking care of it for as long as you're here on this earth?"

I considered what she'd just said. For some reason, it frightened me a little. Worry began nibbling away at my overactive imagination. *For as long as I'm here on this earth? Exactly what did she mean by that? That I was going to fall off the face of the earth one day soon—or maybe that I was going to die or get kidnapped or something?*

I was scaring myself. I decided just to be happy.

"I'll treat it really well," I promised, trying not to visualize myself slipping off the side of the world and falling through space.

I meant it, too. I pledged to myself, right then and there, to keep my Egyptian purse out of harm's way. I wouldn't even bring it in for show-and-tell. There was no way in the world I was going to carry it to church or even take it to school. My class sometimes had peanut butter and jelly for snack, and I'd stick needles in my eyes if one of my friends smudged the precious leather with peanut-butter-covered fingers, even accidentally.

My grandmother reached for the purse and held it in her hands. She looked at it for what felt like a long time. Maybe she was thinking about her trip, about the camels and donkey carts and pyramids and all. Most probably, she was thinking about the power and pull of that continent, about the dawn of civilization and how everything started in Africa. Finally, she spoke.

"Yes, yes, yes," she said, almost speaking to herself. "Mama

thought this little number had your name written all over it."
(A few weeks after our visit, I took her statement literally—
by writing my name on the purse in red ink. I think I did it
because I wanted to make sure people knew that this precious
purse belonged to me and me alone. By writing my name on
it, I didn't think I was defacing it; I was simply making sure
that folks knew that my grandmother loved me enough to
have brought me back this exotic gift from a foreign land. To
this very day, my Egyptian purse lies safely tucked away in
my Forever Box, a little bruised and beat up, but *with me*
nonetheless. If you look closely, the red ink is still clearly
legible. In my second-grade chicken scratch, I'd carefully
written my name: *Kristin Clark*.)

Mama Lilly patted the small space beside her; an invitation for me to come sit close. I moved in quickly, eager to
smell her talcum-powdery grandmother-smell and lean my
head against her shoulder. Her plumpness pleased me to no
end. There was nowhere else I wanted to be.

As evening came, we sat together on the front porch,
rocking gently on her glider. Purple streaks marked the
sky, slowly changing to cobalt blue, then midnight blue,
then, finally, to the black of night. We spoke in hushed
tones. The power of the past seemed to wrap itself around
our shoulders.

Mama Lilly wanted to talk.

And I wanted to listen.

The sounds of nighttime surrounded us. Crickets chirped loudly in the background. Every now and then a car drove past, its tires making swishing sounds on the wet pavement. Mama Lilly spoke of family history, of how her great-grandmother had been a slave. I imagined a beautiful, utterly charming woman who looked just like Mama Lilly—except shackled in chains or maybe being torn away from her children as they were being sold away to a different master.

She didn't go into much more detail, but I had already learned enough about what my people had had to endure: These brave, beautiful women (and men) had come to America in chains and shackles. I'd seen some pictures and read some of the books in the school library (the ones for kids, like about Harriet Tubman and Frederick Douglass and all). I knew that a lot of my ancestors hadn't even survived the trip; many of them died on the way over. I also knew that they'd been forced to lie down in tight rows at the bottom of the boat, in a space so small it reminded me of the first time I ever saw someone in a coffin—at my Uncle Tommy's funeral (and I had nightmares for months afterward). I remember thinking, as I looked at poor, dead Uncle Tommy lying there, *Why in the world would someone have stuffed him into such a tight box—with a lid on it, no less? Is he supposed to spend the rest of his life being stuck underground, without even any space to move around?* Well, that's about as much room as the slaves had on their voyage—which, essentially, was *no* room at all. No room to roll over or sit up or even reach up to scratch your nose if you felt an itch. The only difference, though, was that the slaves were *alive*. They had to eat and breathe in those tight spaces, for weeks on end. At least Uncle Tommy was dead. The slaves were living and breathing . . . kind of like being forced to lie in your own floating coffin.

My eyes itched. My heart battered around in my chest. My past was mingling with my present, and it made my seven-year-old heart swoon in pain and sadness. I reached over for Mama Lilly's hand. Her warmth warmed me. She squeezed my hand, patting it lightly.

I shook my head vigorously, in an effort to rid myself of those horrible images of my foremothers on the auction block, being ripped from the arms of their screaming children as they were being sold away, or lying in their floating coffins. I didn't hear myself whimper, but Mama Lilly certainly must have, because she scooted me closer to her warm body and placed my head gently onto her bosom.

"There, there, honey pie," she murmured down into the crown of my head. "You mustn't cry."

As she stroked my cheeks, more tears appeared. I cried for the great-great-grandfather I never even knew, who'd been forced to stand really, really still—without screaming or making any little noise at all—while he was being whipped. I cried for the children who were my age who'd been snatched away from their mothers and families, never to lay eyes on them again. I cried because I was slowly but surely coming to realize that the world is not all sweetness and generosity and sparkling light; that there *is* darkness sometimes, and that people can and will be cold and cruel to each other, on purpose! I cried at the realization that, even though my insular, neatly packaged little sugarcoated world might have been filled to the brim with love and laughter, a huge chunk of life was not. Large parts of the outside world were hateful and haunting, with real-life monsters that captured and killed and certainly aimed to hurt. My tears wouldn't stop.

I could feel Mama Lilly reaching for her embroidered handkerchief, trying to pull it from the front pocket of her housecoat. I leaned away from her just a tiny bit, to give her room to get the hankie, but I was still crying pretty hard. Even as I cried, I hoped she wasn't getting worried; after all, she was pretty old and there wasn't much she could do with a blubbering seven-year-old in the dead of night. *Please, God, don't let her have a heart attack.* I also prayed that my nose wouldn't start running all over the place, because even though she was my grandmother and I loved her more than applesauce with cinnamon, it still would have been pretty embarrassing if she'd had to wipe it like I was a one-year-old baby. (Thank God she didn't have to.)

After a minute of digging around in her pocket, though, she did find her kerchief (as she called it). As soon as she pulled it out, she leaned in close and started plucking and patting my tearstained face with such tenderness and love that it almost made me start crying all over again. I swear. Life is funny like that. Emotions can definitely get tricky.

This scene on Mama Lilly's porch reminded me very much of the same scene on Mrs. Simpson's porch just two days earlier—the way Mrs. Simpson had so gently and lovingly patted my face dry with her ever-ready dish towel after I had gotten splashed by that speeding Thunderbird as I was crossing the street. The constant tenderness my elderly lady friends displayed toward me was unimaginably comforting. Their collective closeness buoyed my little spirit. It made me feel safe. Connected. Smiled upon from above. Protected from the evil that lurked in the darkened shadows.

In her sweet, floral-scented effort to calm me down, Mama Lilly clucked quietly for a few minutes and patted my face softly with the palm of her hand. When my breathing had normalized and the sniffling had subsided, she began to speak—so softly I just about had to stop breathing to hear her.

"Mama doesn't want you to be sad, baby," she whispered. "But you *should* be aware of the fact that, unfortunately, there is cruelty in the world. People aren't always nice to each other—whether it's one person calling another person a mean name." Immediately, I thought of what Sheila and I had just been through. "Or an entire race of people trying to wipe out another—it's just the sad fact of the matter: Human beings *can* be cruel. Mighty, mighty cruel. And one of our jobs as responsible, civilized human beings—for as long as we're here on this earth—is to do our part to cancel out as much cruelty as we can. Sitting by and letting it happen is simply not an option."

She looked down at me then, but she kept patting my cheeks softly. I never wanted her to stop. Still, the image of my great-great-grandmother, shackled and standing high up on the auction block, trying her mightiest to twist away from the calloused, groping hands of the slave trader, remained riveted in my mind. Even then, what little I knew about slavery, I hated. And I hated it because I couldn't get a grip on why one race of people would want to *own* another race—in the same way I owned the new bag of marbles my sister Noelle had just given me, or my new pair of patent leather church shoes or even my new plaid Western shirt with the fancy pearl buttons from Sears, Roebuck & Co. None of it made any sense. People were supposed to own *things*—not other people.

I looked up at my grandmother, hoping she'd blow away the poisonous pictures that were forming in my mind.

She looked down at me and smiled her sweet, sweet smile.

"Mama knows your mother and father have already talked to you a little about slavery, honey, 'cause they asked my advice about how much they should say, and when."

My mother, seeking advice from her own mother, about how best to communicate with her baby girl about the ugliness of slavery?

I imagined my parents, sitting at Mama Lilly's kitchen table, concerned looks on their faces, as they probed and prodded about the best way to teach me the life lesson that people were sometimes cruel and hateful and bigoted and ugly; that they sometimes enslaved each other and whipped each other and sold each other away like cattle. And there we were—three generations, all trying to make sense of an historical atrocity that had affected each of us powerfully, personally, and in profoundly different ways.

"Mama already knows you know a little bit about this painful part of our history, and I strongly believe it's better that you learn about it from your family first. I say this, honey, because I know that the history books you'll read— or may have already read—have a strange way of twisting up the real facts into little knots that are sometimes hard for young minds to untangle. What happened to our people is what happened to our own bloodline—it lives and breathes and pulsates within our own veins. Mama's not telling you to ignore the history books, but I *am* telling you—just like your mama and daddy have told you—to feel it within your own spirit. Let it burn into your own mind, and your own memory. And, more than anything, you must *learn* from these horrible lessons."

She rubbed my arm and spoke again.

"Why do you think it's important for us to learn about the atrocities of our past?"

Lord God almighty. She couldn't actually be waiting for me to answer such a question, could she? I knew she considered me to be a smart seven-year-old, but this was bordering on ridiculous.

So I just stayed silent. I just hoped and prayed that she'd answer her own question. How in the world would *I* know the reason we'd want to remember such a poisonous part of our past? I hadn't a clue.

An uncomfortable silence began growing between us, like a stink plant or poison ivy. It didn't feel good at all. *Was she actually waiting for an answer?*

After what felt like about a thousand hours of just sitting there together, she finally did answer her own question— and her voice was no longer a whisper, but a forceful declaration:

"We try to remember it *forever*, so that nothing like it will ever happen again." It was a lesson I'd remember for the rest of my life, in increasingly sophisticated levels of awareness as I grew older. Mama Lilly had been exactly right, on many different levels: The more aware we are of our past mistakes, the less likely it is that we'll repeat them.

I wondered, then, as we sat together on the porch that evening, whether there was a deeper reason behind her bringing that beautiful purse for me, all the way from Egypt.

I wondered, as we rocked together, whether she'd wanted to remind me that, although our people were once kings and queens and had actually given birth to civilized society, we'd also faced unimaginable atrocities and indignities— indignities such as slavery that would leave us bent, but not broken. Weakened, but not paralyzed. (Perhaps that's why one of her favorite sayings was always, "It doesn't matter if you stumble and fall; take pride in the fact that you shake yourself off and *get back up!*")

I remembered again what she'd told me the word *Cairo* meant in Arabic: "victorious." And I sensed that "victorious" meant courageous. Brave. A winner, no matter what the circumstance.

That my people have survived such pain and indignity over the course of history, only to grow stronger and wiser as a result, certainly makes me feel *victorious*. And my grandmother's urgings to learn more about not just my own history but the history of the entire world around me helped open up my spirit and widen my spiritual embrace. She helped me realize that, no matter what the color of our skin, we are all connected to each other by simple virtue of the fact that we all inhabit this same planet, we all breathe the same air together, and we all occupy a singularly unique and wonderfully collective space within this one universe.

Shortly after that powerful but somewhat painful evening, I began to pray for increased awareness and understanding

about the world around me. I knew full well that what Mama
Lilly had taught me that evening—about knowing our history so we can avoid future mistakes—was right on target,
but it was still a bit unsettling.

My prayer was this: *Please, God, help me understand why
some people are mean and hateful. Shower me with knowledge
about compassion and universal love and how to move away from
hatred. If there are lessons I need to learn, Lord, teach them to me
so that I may help bring love and tolerance back into this world—
not just for me, but for all races, everywhere. Even though I'm
only seven, guide me in a way that helps make this world a better
place.*

I believe it was the first prayer I'd ever uttered that actually expanded beyond and leapfrogged over the people in
my immediate sphere of influence (my family, Mrs. Simpson, Miss Miriam, and all of my friends at school) and actually included the larger world around us. It was my first
spiritual plea for compassion and empathy and for guidance
and it signaled to me a maturation of spirit and a deepening
of heart. Mama Lilly was the woman who helped nudge me
to that spiritual place, and I'll always be grateful to her for
teaching me to pray for the wider world around me. Still, I
continued my prayer for deeper understanding.

Eventually—as always—God answered.

About a year later, something happened.

For weeks on end, I'd been noticing Mother reading a

certain book. Usually when she read, you could tell she was enjoying it deeply; she would either curl up in the armchair in our living room, or maybe sit out on our front porch, basking in the sunlight, completely transported to some foreign and exotic world by the words within her book.

But not with *this* book.

Whenever she'd read this particular book, her facial expression took on a serious, sometimes pained expression. Worry wrinkled the space between her eyebrows. And when she read this book, she never curled up, but sat ramrod straight, at either the kitchen table or the card table where she did all of her writing. I'd even watch as she highlighted certain sections, shaking her head in disgust or disappointment. It was also clear that she didn't want me to come anywhere near her while she read—the first time Mother had *ever* spurned my presence.

So I took to sneaking. I took to peeking. I took to snatching quick glances at the words whenever I passed by, trying to appear completely disinterested.

One afternoon, though, Mother got careless—and I made my move.

The moment she placed her book down to get a glass of water from the kitchen, I pounced upon it like a caged tiger. I knew I didn't have much time, so I worked quickly. Most of the words were difficult to decipher, so quick as lightning, I snatched up the nearest pencil and a piece of scrap paper.

I wrote down some of the words she'd already highlighted, knowing that I could look them up later in our dog-eared Webster's Dictionary or our wonderful set of Encyclopedia Britannica—the *complete* set, I might add, or maybe even out of one of our World Books. (Our household was filled to the brim with excellent reference books, thanks to Mother.)

Even as I wrote down the words, I could feel the hairs at the nape of my neck begin to stand at full attention. My stomach rumbled. My hands were perspiring so heavily I could barely hold the pencil; my fingers were shaking so badly I could barely read my own writing. But I didn't have time to feel guilty about the intrusion. I somehow felt something larger was at stake.

As I wrote down the words, my heart and hands seemed to freeze. Time slowed. And worse yet, I could hear Mother placing her drinking glass back into the sink, preparing to head back into the living room. Quickly but ever so carefully, I returned the book to the precise position in which she'd left it.

I barely made it out of the room in time.

As I peered through the living room doors, I could actually see tears sparkling in my mother's eyes. I decided I hated this book, and I hated what it was doing to the most important person in my entire life.

It was time to get to work.

Later that evening, when everyone else was occupied

with their own projects and activities, I made my way to the television room, where we kept most of our books in these beautiful, built-in bookshelves that Mother had had constructed just for us, which still exist in that house to this very day. These wonderful books opened up worlds we'd never see and brought us face to face with facts and figures we never could have imagined. As I looked up each entry, my nervousness increased. It might have been the first time I'd ever experienced, on a personal level, the definition of the word *dread*.

I knew no one in the family would think it unusual that I was looking up specific words. Mother and Daddy constantly encouraged all us kids to seek knowledge from reference books as often as possible—but I knew I had to be careful to conceal my reactions, if there were any.

Slowly, but surely, using every reference book we had in the house, I looked up each word.

Auschwitz.

My breathing slowed until it was just about stopped.

Concentration camps.

Bitter bile began to rise up in my throat.

Hitler, Adolf.

Holocaust.

Gas chambers.

Gestapo.

Although I had trouble understanding some of the

concepts, I was beginning to understand. And the more I understood, the less I wanted to read. But I was having trouble reading anyway for my vision was blurred by my tears, making it virtually impossible for me to see.

I ran to my bedroom and cried myself to sleep.

❧

I AWOKE the next morning to Mother's soft kisses covering my cheeks and eyelids and nose.

"Morning, Beauty," she whispered. But something caught in her voice. I could hear it the second she spoke. *Something was off-balance.*

I sat up and noticed right off that she was holding something in her hands. Rubbing my eyes, I peered closer. *Jesus MaryandJoseph.*

It was the list of words I'd looked up the night before. I must have dropped it on the floor before I fell asleep.

The jig was up.

"Sweetheart, you know I love you and I would never intentionally mean to harm you, right?"

Even that she would ask such a question set my soul on fire. I didn't know whether to stand up or throw up. I didn't say a word.

She took me into her warm embrace, rocking me gently. Suddenly, the words exploded forth.

"I'm sorry, Mama. I just wanted to know what you were

reading that was upsetting you so much. I didn't mean to spy and I didn't mean to snoop, but I was worried because it was making you so sad. That's why I did it, Mama. That's why I looked those words up."

She regarded me momentarily, her eyebrows knitted, either out of intense love for her child or because she was just so filled with anger and disgust that she couldn't speak.

Fortunately for me, it was the former.

"Sweetheart, I never ever want to hurt you. But there are certain things that you're just not ready to *know*—not just yet."

She shook her head sadly.

"For heaven's sake . . . *I'm* just now getting up the courage to really teach *myself*, in full detail, about what happened during that horrible time. For all these years, I've just been too much of a coward to read anything more detailed than a newspaper article or a short magazine piece. Even today, sweetheart, I still can't get my mind around what happened . . . It's called the Holocaust, if you want to know.

"This book I'm reading is the first full account I've read about that nightmarish time, honey—and you know how much I love to read. I just couldn't bring my heart or my mind to open that part of history back up again. It hurt too much—and I didn't want it to hurt you."

We looked at each other, silent. I'd never heard her speak that way—so open, so vulnerable, so emotionally honest.

She continued, "You know your father and I have always

taught you children that knowledge is power. We still believe that, and we always will. But I don't want to lay something so heavy on your young, little heart that it breaks into a million pieces . . . and what happened during the Holocaust could break anyone's spirit. I was going to wait until you were a little older . . . but looks like you beat me to the punch."

Holocaust.

The very mention of that word brought us together in a closer, much more urgent embrace. My spirit felt raw. Hers probably felt raw *and* betrayed that I had snuck behind her back to get a look at the very thing that she was trying to protect me from. But I had something I needed to say.

"Remember about a year ago, when I spent the night with Mama Lilly and she gave me that pretty purse from Egypt?"

Mother nodded, her gaze never leaving mine.

"Well, she told me on that very same night that she thought that it was time I learned about some of the awful things that have happened in the world . . . She said that it's kind of my *responsibility* to know—for everyone to know—so that we won't make the same stupid mistakes twice."

I was sputtering now. Tears were pooling up, threatening to overflow. Still, I rambled on.

"I know that you and Daddy asked her advice about when to tell me about slavery—and I know that she believes I should *not* be so sheltered from the bad stuff that has happened in the world."

And then, a few last lines before I broke into tears: "I'm *not* a baby. I deserve to know—not just about slavery but about everything. Things like slavery and the Holocaust *happened*, Ma. It happened right in this very world we live in. I've read about some of this in the school library. I *love* it when we read books like *Black Beauty* together, Ma, but there are real-life books that explain history and how things happen in the world. I want to know, too! So tell me once again: Why is it fair for *you* to know—*and not me*?"

We both sat on the bed, shocked into silence. Finally she spoke.

"Part of what you say is right, Beauty. You *should* know the history of the world you live in. It's your right and your privilege. But as your mother, I reserve the right to tell you the things you need to know when I think you're ready for them. However, because you beat me to the punch this time, we might as well talk now."

I could tell she was a little mad about my spying on her, and about meddling in her and Daddy's parental decisions and child-rearing philosophies. But I was more interested in the notion that she was actually about to share with me a part of history that not only changed the lives of all those millions of innocent people who were killed (as well as the lives of their surviving loved ones), but redefined the very notion of good and bad, and right and wrong.

We spoke well into the morning. I cried, and she cried. I

could tell she was still holding back a lot of information, but I knew it was out of love, and I knew that one day, when I was older, she'd let me find out for myself.

After that, Mother read her book openly. She still cried as she read (keeping a handkerchief tucked in her fist), but she read nonetheless—no matter how painful. Today, her book sits not in my Forever Box, but in my home library. It sits as a stark reminder—and a sorrowful tribute—to the millions of innocent men, women, and children who were so mercilessly led to their deaths during one of the darkest periods in history. And whenever I open its pages, I think of Mother— of her tears, her rage, and her driving desire to shield me from the truth until she thought my heart was ready to withstand its raw and ravaging ugliness.

The book: *While Six Million Died.*

The lesson: People hate. People kill. People can be unspeakably cruel to each other.

But out of darkness, comes the light. Out of pain, comes power and perseverance. Out of struggle—whether it's the sinful nature of slavery, the horrors of the Holocaust, or something as pure and innocent as a child's fear of the dark—comes gradual awakening.

In a very real way, it was that afternoon spent with Mama Lilly that spurred me on to spy on Mother and to recognize the importance of being aware of what's happening around us.

Decades later, when my own children were right around

the same age as I was then—about seven or eight—they were exposed, in a very general sense, to parts of our history that can never be erased. Yes, the knowledge was initially unsettling to them, but it is infinitely better to know than not.

Ignorance is *never* bliss. It's tragic.

❧

EVEN through my tears—on that magical yet emotionally draining evening as I sat with my grandmother—I knew that my life had been changed forever. And it was Mama Lilly who'd opened the door of my heart to include people of all colors, cultures, and backgrounds. She was a trailblazer, that woman.

A woman ahead of her time.

❧

DEEPLY committed to her church, St. Philips Lutheran Church, Mama Lilly loved the Lord with passion and power. She was also a generous, compassionate woman who gave of herself freely and without hesitation—particularly to those who were in need. Whenever she encountered a hungry person, she provided a warm, home-cooked meal. If a neighbor or friend fell down on their luck, she'd offer up whatever financial relief she could afford. She cherished her family with a fierce, fiery pride. The memory of her warm smile and twinkling eyes will always burn brightly in my mind.

Without a doubt, my grandmother Mary Elizabeth Sorsby was a maverick.

She was also a capable, compassionate businesswoman and entrepreneur.

Many years earlier, before I was born, she started her own successful business. Quite early in her adult life, she'd worked for an elderly, scholarly doctor, and before he died, he passed along to her a secret formula that would change her life forever—and enhance the lives of countless others. It was a formula that he'd developed after many years of hard research—and he'd passed it along to no one but Mama Lilly. It was a formula that, when followed with the utmost precision, created a medicine that warded off the common cold, helped reduce arthritic pain, and successfully fought off many other commonplace maladies.

My grandmother's working laboratory was located in a downstairs room in her basement—actually, a second kitchen—which I always remember as being shockingly clean, neat, and organized. Empty, sterilized bottles stood in tidy rows, waiting to be filled to the brim with the magical elixir—a clear liquid with a very powerful, pungent smell. Labels were stacked in neat piles on the countertop, waiting to be affixed to the medicine bottles before they were shipped out to drugstores throughout the city. Friends and family members from near and far swore by her medicine, which she had named "Relief." (I remember clearly, as a child, making a quick stop with my father into the Davis Cut Rate store in downtown Detroit, seeing the familiar bottles of Relief lined neatly on the store's shelves, and how my little heart filled up with pride.)

Mama Lilly relied heavily on her children and grand-children to assist in the medicine-making process. To this very day, every one of my older siblings holds clear, concise memories of assisting Mama Lilly in her laboratory—but she would never *ever* permit any of us to tamper with the actual formula or the liquid itself. She was meticulous almost to a fault, and she took her job as medicine-maker very seri-ously. On a regular basis, she'd ship boxes upon boxes of Relief to drugstores and to faithful, long-standing custom-ers, who clamored for the miracle elixir from points near and far. Needless to say, every one of her family members (children, grandchildren, great-grandchildren) kept at *least* one bottle of Relief close at hand, either in the medicine cab-inets or on their kitchen shelves. Admittedly, it *tasted* like dirty bathwater with cayenne pepper sprinkled on top, but it healed and helped like nobody's business.

Hers was not a fly-by-night, under-the-table enterprise by any means. For years, she interfaced with the Food and Drug Administration, who monitored the medicine quite closely. One important requirement from the FDA, as I remember it, was that her medicine be referred to as a "home remedy"—rather than the established, factory-tested brands from the major pharmaceutical companies. This technical requirement prevented stores from placing the actual bottles alongside the other, better-known cold remedies, but Mama Lilly pressed ahead nonetheless.

On a regular basis, Mama Lilly would descend into her basement to create fresh batches of the medicine. She had the secret formula memorized by heart, of course, but she was always extremely careful and precise with her measurements. For her, it was an exact science. Human health was at stake. She also prayed over every bottle before it went out, blessing each one individually.

Every so often, she'd allow me to join her in her laboratory. I remember not only the laboratory, but the entire process itself feeling very scientific—and extremely somber. From time to time, my grandmother would even allow me to adhere the labels onto the bottles—but her standards were exacting and extremely strict. If I incorrectly adhered even one label—whether it was crooked or, heaven forbid, upside down—she'd stop me dead in my tracks and promptly send me back upstairs to watch cartoons or play in the backyard.

She was a wizard and a wonder, my grandmother. As I mentioned before, most definitely a woman well ahead of her time. How bountifully blessed I am to have shared with her the same familial blood.

It was Mama Lilly who taught me that women and

business can and do mix together quite beautifully. She was frugal, fearless, and as forward-looking as any woman I've ever known.

Neither her gender nor the color of her skin were impediments; if anything, they spurred her into action with a ferocity that was rare even then, in the mid 1960s. Like my mother, she strongly believed in the notion that women everywhere, black and white, young and old, should be treated with the same amount of deference and respect as men. She believed that once you put your mind to it, anything was possible—and that no barriers existed that could not be overcome. ("With God," she'd often recite from Matthew 19:26, "all things are possible.")

Mama Lilly "lived in the moment" long before "living in the moment" became trendy and politically correct. Utterly unwilling to worry about the troubles and travails that may be facing us down the road, this wonderful woman always welcomed each new day as a glorious gift, and she embraced the *promise* of tomorrow like a long-awaited friend. It was Mama Lilly who taught me to surrender my fear, give over my anxiety, and release all the uncertainties about the future to a Power far, far greater than ourselves. Her motto as it concerned life and living: "Don't ever worry about tomorrow—because God has been there since yesterday." It is a motto I live by today. I carry it wrapped in and around my spirit at all times.

Too many women, far too often, get caught up and forced down by the prospect of failure, of freedom, and of striking out in a world that is at times unwelcoming and unfair. It was Mama Lilly who first taught me, at the tender age of seven, that we cannot afford to mire ourselves in the mud and muck of negative thinking.

Without a doubt, Mary Elizabeth Sorsby blazed exciting new trails and set higher standards of excellence not only for her family, but for every person her life touched. To her, the prospect of "tomorrow" was a beacon—*not* a burden. Until the end of her life, she remained undaunted by challenge. And when the going became particularly rough, she would never *ever* slip into the shadows or wring her hands helplessly in fear or frustration. (Another one of her favorite passages comes from Matthew 6:27: "Who of you, by worrying, can add a single hour to your life?")

Yes, indeed, my grandmother cherished all of her yesterdays, lived fully and without apology within every minute of every day, and welcomed the arrival of tomorrow with emotional spunk and spiritual vigor. Positive thinking was built into her character; it abided deep, deep down in her soul. And, perhaps without even knowing it, she passed this positivity on down to the generations who came after her, to every one of her children, grandchildren, great-grands. Like a steaming locomotive, her path was straight and true: She passed the best and brightest parts of herself directly down to every one of my siblings, to each of my sibling's children, and to the new generations after that.

Her spirit will live forever among us—long after we have sung our last song and cried our last tear. I uplift and honor this miraculous woman with all my heart and soul—and I know that, without her, there would be no Mother, and without Mother, there would be no me. And certainly, as it stands to reason, I could not have brought my own precious progeny into this world had it not been for those wondrous women who came before me.

So it is these women I thank. It is these women who have entrusted me with their mementos and their memories. The mere fact that these miraculous women existed at all is a gift of such great magnitude that it takes my breath away. And being breathless—in this context, anyway—is a wonderful, wonderful feeling.

A child's Egyptian purse and a mother's sad-but-true book on an ugly part of our history are two more of the precious treasures in my home that will live forever. And when I reach into my Forever Box to pull out the Egyptian purse my grandmother brought me from Cairo so many decades ago, I remember not only the true meaning of "victorious," but the life lessons my grandmother taught me. Lessons about the importance of familiarizing ourselves with the history of the world; with our civic and moral responsibility to do whatever we can to stop the vicious, repetitive cycle of man's inhumanity to man, and to celebrate the fact that women can be equally as competitive and entrepreneurial in business and finance as their male counterparts.

And to think that the stories and the life lessons attached to them are kept alive by, among other things, a child's small leather purse.

❧

SINGLEHANDEDLY, during our special overnight visit that weekend, but also in the years that followed, my grandmother had drawn me a picture of what "forever" looks like. She'd taught me that forever has depth, breadth, and specific dimensions. Forever is not some vague, vacuous notion at all, but rather a touchable, tangible thing that directly connects us to our larger selves and celebrates the fact that our lives and the things we carry with us through life are not random at all, but intimately interconnected. Forever is made up of real people and real things.

Throughout her life, she taught me that history is real and can oftentimes be ugly, but that we have a larger responsibility, to ourselves and each other, not only to educate ourselves about the universe around us—whether it's by expanding our own horizons and trying to see as much of the world as possible with our own eyes—but also to do our part to actively halt cruelty and evil whenever and wherever we see it.

A quick glance at my Egyptian purse catapults me back to that evening on the porch with my grandmother, reminding me of the lessons she taught me about compassion toward others and the limitless potential that every woman should enjoy—whether they chair a board in bustling Manhattan or work the night shift at the local factory.

Whatever our personal circumstance, we must always embrace the individual and collective belief that we are, all of us, one and the same. And although our circumstances may differ, we should not only recognize but celebrate the fact that we are not traveling on our journeys alone. We are, all of us, inextricably bound together by faith and by friendship. We are the sum of our own positive, collective totality.

There are other life lessons as well, lessons about the importance of and sheer joy that comes with *throwing* open the doors and windows of opportunity, and pushing forward into uncharted territory, where no man (or woman) has ever gone before. To think new thoughts. Embrace new beliefs. Anchor ourselves and our spirits with the collective knowledge that, no, we do not walk in this world alone and lonely. We are *bound*. Bound together in a wide, loving embrace that can *always* be widened to include others.

And if I never ever make it to that ancient, bustling city of Cairo in my lifetime, that's okay with me. Why? Because it already exists within the dimly lit corners of my own memory. This knowledge lifts me up, strengthens my spirit, and makes me feel—for lack of a better word—simply *victorious*.

Yes indeed. A piece of Egypt lives right there in the darkened recesses of my Forever Box.

And so does Mama Lilly.

TOUCHING FOREVER

— ❧ —

I HAVE FIGURED OUT many different ways of touching forever.

Some methods are simple; others require a bit more effort.

The concept of forever can exist within the elegant simplicity of a family name. From the moment they were born, for example, my two children—now responsible, respectful adults—have carried with them the mantle of "memory-maker." How? Simply by their given names.

My son, Lonnie Paul, is named after his paternal great-grandfather (whose name was Lonnie), his great-uncle (whose name was Paul), and his father (whose name is also Lonnie Paul). Similarly, my daughter's name, Mary Elizabeth (or some close variation) has survived within my family blood-line for many generations. My great-grandmother's name was Mary, my grandmother's name was Mary Elizabeth, and my mother was also Mary Elizabeth. It is my daughter, yet another Mary Elizabeth, who now proudly carries the familial torch. And it brings me untold joy, pride, and a sense of generational continuity to already know (because she's told me) that, when it's time, my daughter will name *her* daughter the same name as well. As a budding memory-maker herself, it has long been a solid part of her familial plan.

A relatively simple but lasting decision such as child-naming, then, can create historical connectivity and can assure the continuation of family lineage. I am certain that both of my children are happy and very proud to bask in the bright light of those who came before them—and not in their shadows, either, but toe to toe. Head to head.

Sadly, Mother left this earth before she could reach out and touch Mary Elizabeth's soft brown hair or play patty-cake with her in the warm afternoon sun. But my grown girl is intimately aware of her grandmother's existence. Both of their spirits are inexorably intertwined. One could even make the figurative claim that these two wondrous women have met before, on a spiritual level.

Similarly, Lonnie Paul was just six months old when Mother died, and not that much older when my father passed away a few years later.

The beauty here, however, is that although my own progeny never had the opportunity to know my parents in any tangible or intimate sense, there still exists between them a very comfortable familiarity nonetheless.

Keeping a Forever Box helps nurture this all-important process of preservation and continuity. Being a memory-maker binds us to something infinitely larger than ourselves and our own individual circumstance. When we can purposefully dust off the cobwebbed memories of the loved ones who came long before us, we play an important role in fitting the disparate pieces of our familial puzzle together to create a clearer, more concise picture of our collective pasts.

Every time my children open the Forever Box, they can reach in and pull out tiny treasures and beautiful baubles that represent, in a very real way, the most positive pieces of their *own* past—a past, I should add, that they would simply be unable to see or touch or feel had it not been so purposefully preserved. It connects them to something larger than themselves, and it helps them make sense of the swirling, turbulent daily world around them.

For my children, then—and for yours, if you decide to make the life-changing decision to become a memory-maker in your own right—the past is not only prologue; it's the promise of being able to reach back into yesterday to hear the stories, learn the life lessons, and preserve the principles of our ancestors who are now long gone. We have it in our individual and collective power, then, to ever so tenderly coax our special memories out of their darkened corners, allowing them to come bursting forth like bright, brilliant rays of sunshine. Doing so helps us know who we are, and where we're going. It helps those generations who'll come after us to center themselves and walk in that bright light of illumination that comes with increased self-awareness and deepened historical understanding.

Nurturing such self-awareness and connectivity helps my children weave together—into one, whole cloth—their past, their present, *and* their future by reminding them that the fast-moving world around them is not a random world at all, but solidly, meaningfully rooted in personal history and familial pride.

Not only this, but I make the sustained and deliberate effort to steep into their spirits the abiding awareness that, if they are truly to become memory-makers in their own right, they must arm themselves with a sense of personal responsibility and commitment.

"Take good care of your things," I often whispered to them throughout their childhood—precisely the same six simple words my Mother whispered to me throughout so much of my own youth.

Take good care of your things.

Nothing less will do.

❧

O*N* any given afternoon or quiet evening (unfortunately, not often enough), my family comes together and gathers around our solid, beautiful Forever Box. If we want to pull from the past, we carefully open the hinged lid, bring out a bauble, and invite the magic to begin. If, on the other hand, my children want to make personal "deposits" of their own, we've had to create new, additional space, if only out of sheer physical necessity. And as both of them have evolved over the years into conscientious keepers of their own keepsakes, so, too, have their instincts to select the treasures they intend on preserving in a careful, purposeful manner.

My children are now memory-makers in their own right. What joy! What blessed assurance! The knowledge that yet another successive generation can now pull the past around its shoulders—and wear it like a protective cloak—brings me untold happiness and spiritual relief.

And if my life ended tomorrow, or even at this very moment, I know that I'll leave *this* earth armed with the comforting knowledge that life doesn't stop when we die. If anything, from a religious, spiritual, and symbolic perspective, it's really only just begun.

Such knowledge presents a study in contrasts:

My ability to successfully preserve the past showers me with feelings of calm, often when I'm in the midst of chaos.

It instills in my spirit an abiding sense of comfort, often when I'm in the throes of emotional pain.

It covers me with a sense of continued spiritual connectivity, often when I feel overwhelmed, isolated, alienated, or hopeless.

❧

My daughter is not at all daunted by the prospect of stepping into the role of becoming the family's keeper of keepsakes once I've gone on away from here. My son, on the other hand, tends to shake such sentimentality right off his shoulders—which is neither good nor bad; but it does mean that his own personal "deposits" into our box are far less frequent. (Not surprisingly, it's been the females in my family, far more often than the males, who have historically carried the memories through generations. It is my belief that women, traditionally and habitually, instinctively embrace their historical role as memory-keepers within a family. More often than not, we are the lamplight that leads the way when the pages of our collective family histories grow dim and difficult to decipher.)

As for me, I will always remember the magic and mystery that crackles in the air around us whenever we open the lid and bring to the light of day the treasured trinkets of our past. And it is my fervent prayer that my children will remember these moments as well, with equal amounts of clarity and conviction.

To be sure, stepping into the role of memory-maker requires emotional energy. Assuming such a role also requires a certain degree of spiritual commitment. And the ability to preserve and protect our long-lost familial memories requires daily dedication and a heightened sense of self, place, and purpose.

ᆼᄼ

ONE gray winter afternoon many years ago, when my Mary Elizabeth was in the first or second grade, she and I sat down together to pluck memories. School was closed because of a sudden and severe snowstorm the night before, so our moments together that afternoon seemed leisurely and languid. My intention on that snowy afternoon was to show her pieces of her past that she'd never laid eyes on—and I realized, even then, that this would be her first experience with the symbolism and significance of being transported back through time.

This would be the first time mother and daughter would deliberately open the hinged lid, reach down inside, and pluck the precious baubles from the box. It would be her maiden voyage, her first journey into the faraway but real-life world of yesterday, to that magical place where time, place, smell, touch, and sight all looped over onto themselves and generations long gone stepped quietly into the bright light of *today*.

I was preparing my baby girl to reach out and touch forever.

She's old enough now, Beauty, I could hear my mother whisper as her maternal spirit moved in beside me, lingering close. I could almost feel the softness of Mother's hands guiding mine as I prepared to escort my daughter back to a time that actually predated her own existence. Mary Elizabeth sat quietly, patiently, an expression of mild curiosity flashing across her face.

The time had come.

Mother's spiritual urgings had been right on target: my gorgeous little girl was, indeed, ready to reach out and pull in her past. She was about seven years old at the time, and as she looked up at me expectantly, my heart pounded and my breathing became shallow.

The moment upon us was both significant and symbolic: It would represent one of the first times in her young life that she would be introduced to the physical memory of Mother.

"There's something very important I want to show you, baby," I said quietly, trying valiantly not to let the tremor in my voice betray my emotionalism.

Mother's presence became even more powerful at that moment, lingering so closely now that I could almost feel the freshly starched cotton of her dress—that very same polka-dot sundress she'd worn decades earlier, when she and I had reminisced together during that long-ago summer thunderstorm. Time was folding over onto itself. My breathing continued to come in short, shallow bursts.

Show her, Beauty. Tell her. Make sure she listens carefully as you speak, and let her hold it in her own little hands. I'm right here with you, sweetheart. In fact, I never really left.

By then, my tears were pooling, threatening to overflow into tiny rivulets down my cheeks. I blinked them away. I didn't want Mary Elizabeth to become worried at the sight of her mother in tears. (As we sat together on that wintry afternoon, with the snow outside blanketing everything around us in a thick, comfortable cushion, I knew that my tears would worry her mind rather than warm her heart. So I forced myself to pull it together.)

Still, I was nervous. My hands were shaking ever so slightly. A faint sheen of perspiration formed on my forehead and in the hollow above my upper lip. Willing myself to calm down, I reached for the box, talking softly the whole while.

"I want you to see this, sweetheart."

Carefully removing the object from its protective covering, I leaned toward my daughter and placed it gently into her hands.

"Whose is this, Mom?" she asked through a slight lisp, since two of her front teeth were missing.

I closed my eyes momentarily, praying fervently. *Thank You, Lord, for guiding us toward this shining moment. Thank You for leading us to this place that is our past. Thank You for letting us touch forever.*

At that very moment, I fully understood and absorbed the rationale behind my keeping a Forever Box at all: Not only did I painstakingly preserve the baubles and trinkets for sentimental reasons, but also for a shining moment such as this—when generational spans converge, and when we are finally able to witness the rare and wonderful coming together of past, present, and future.

Suddenly, and for the first time, I'd come face-to-face with that moment: the magic moment, when everything converges. I was no longer the receiver of treasured trinkets and beautiful old baubles—but the *giver*. Just as Miss Miriam had passed along to me her dainty perfume bottle, and in the same way that Mrs. Simpson had given to me her precious teacups, it was my turn to pass along the past. I smiled at the memory of Miss Miriam digging through her steamer trunk and pulling out an evening bag for me that, to this very day, lies safely tucked away in the cedar. My heart leaps with pride when I pull out my Egyptian purse, and I remember that magical afternoon when my grandmother gave it to me. Now, suddenly, the tables had turned. Yes, indeed. I was the giver, and my daughter was the recipient.

The changing of the guards.

And the peaceful, personal realization that, while my time on this earth is finite and limited, my loving legacy is not.

I cleared my throat, quickly swiping away a tear. I wanted to answer my daughter's question, clearly and directly.

"It was my mother's," I whispered, placing it into her hands with tender care. Pride and passion pushed itself into the air around us.

Mary Elizabeth turned the precious piece around and around in her hands, a lazy smile dancing a little samba across her face.

I leaned down to plant a sweet, brown Hershey-chocolate mother-kiss smack in the middle of her forehead. Time stood still, pulled us backward into the past, and catapulted us into the future—all at the same time.

Placing the flats of my palms on either side of her warm, lovely cheeks, I peered down into her eyes and began the story.

"It was your grandmother's," I said, pride dripping from my voice.

I paused, tears stinging my eyes. "It was her favorite church hat."

❧

As we sat together on the sofa that afternoon, snowflakes began to fall again. Mary Elizabeth readjusted her small body so that she was nestled comfortably in my arms.

"Tell me more about the church hat," she demanded demurely, clearly intrigued and appropriately reverent (as reverent as a seven-year-old can be, anyway).

Immediately and automatically, my mind skittered side-ways, straight back to that rainy afternoon with Mother, when I'd begged her to tell me the church hat story just *one more time!* While I absently stroked my daughter's arm, I smiled at the memory of me and Mother sitting together in our living room on that gray, rainy day, thunder rolling in the distance. I even remembered Kaboodle, our family cat, and how he'd slithered around the table that afternoon, sitting sphinx-like and genuinely interested in Mother's story, too.

On that special day, literally a lifetime ago, my mother's voice rang out as clear as a bell. Her church hat story, to my little ears, filled my soul and my imagination with the vivid, visual details of her rich experience.

Sitting there that afternoon with my own daughter, I pulled the parallels in around me, smiling to myself: I'd been seven-going-on-eight when my mother shared with me her church hat story, just as my daughter was precisely the same age as I was now sharing the story with her.

And like my daughter, I, too, had been so thirsty for my mother's touch and for the soft lilt of her voice that it literally took my breath away.

On that snowy afternoon, I knew that my baby wanted—needed—to be pulled back into the past, and I knew that I was the one to do the pulling.

We sat together, mother and child, talking into the

afternoon, as the snow outside fell in big, fat flakes. As I spoke, I watched closely as her gaze brushed past me and reached up to the window above us, so that she could watch the falling snow—much the same way I'd gazed at the heavy gray sky on that rainy afternoon with Mother.

And as we sat together, I wondered if she could feel my heart rhythms, in the same way I'd felt Mother's. *Please, God, let her feel my rhythm at this very moment. Let my mother's church hat story nestle deeply in her heart. Let the power of her grandmother's story heighten her sense of direct connection to the world around her. Please—let my baby girl reach out and touch forever.*

Mary Elizabeth held the navy blue hat in her hands the entire time I told the story. When we were finished, I showed her how to wrap the hat all by herself and return it carefully to its rounded, floral box.

On that day, Mother came to visit us both.

On that day, two beautiful people named Mary Elizabeth reached across time and finally introduced themselves, spirit to spirit.

How blessed we are when we are lucky enough to witness the time continuum fold over onto itself and link together, one generation with the next! The process is almost mathematical in its precision, and it sets into motion a divine and mysterious life principle: *As people die, others are born, and thus what was shifting remains constant.*

And if that's not about the best definition of "forever,"
then I simply don't know what is.

∾

SEVERAL weeks after that magical afternoon with my daughter, Mother's spirit stepped in quietly yet again. Mary Elizabeth and I were sitting by the Forever Box, laughing quietly
at a joke she'd just told.

Knock knock.

Who's there?

Anita.

Anita who?

*Anita borrow your pencil, please! I have a poem I want to
write!*

As we laughed together, I admired her crooked little
snaggletoothed smile, wondering idly when her new front
teeth would come in. When she laughed, everyone around
her laughed, because the sound was so pure. So uninhib-
ited. So deliciously heartfelt, like bubbles chasing one
another.

There we were, mother and daughter, sitting shoulder to
shoulder next to the Forever Box. Magic swirled in the air
around us. Kinetic energy bounced and zinged this way and
that. Mary Elizabeth had just finished placing her own
newly acquired "First Place" blue ribbon into the box (for
being the fastest runner at school), and our mood was jovial.

It was at about that moment I felt Mother's spiritual presence brush against my body, light as a feather.

You've taught her well, Beauty. Now she's ready to see more. Reach in and show her more pieces of her past. She gets it! Tell another of our special stories. Help her make sense of the world around her. It's time.

I listened to Mother's spiritual urging, vitally aware of the magnitude of the moment. Again, Mother was right on target. It was the perfect time to pluck another piece of our past from the darkened depths of our box and share it, mother to daughter. My ears tingled. Beads of perspiration formed on my forearms. I wiggled my toes.

"Remember your grandmother's church hat?" I asked, gently prodding, watching to see if her facial expression shifted even slightly—from amusement about her recent joke to genuine curiosity about what was to come.

"Yep, I do, Mom. It's wrapped up in the hatbox right here," she answered, pointing toward the floral box. "I remember the story—about how the store wouldn't even let her try that first hat on, so she made one for herself."

Although I might have been wrong (but I don't think so), I was fairly certain that I'd heard the slightest pull of pride in my daughter's voice as she recounted how her grandmother, all those many years ago, had been treated so coldly by the saleslady in the department store, simply because of the color of her skin.

How relieved and comforted I felt to know that she'd remembered the hat story to its finest detail. And in a flash of fresh awareness, I realized at that moment that the church hat story would burn as brightly as the North Star for generations to come. That is the power that comes from preserving pieces of our familial past.

"*She gets it*"—precisely what Mother's spirit had told me moments before. Thank the Lord. She gets it.

She continued gazing at me expectantly, waiting to be shown yet another artifact from the box. Her innate curiosity pleased me to no end. It made my soul smile. I could feel the time continuum looping over onto itself again and again; that circular, universal rhythm that reminds us that we are—all of us—a vital, visible part of something infinitely larger than our own solitary existence, and that our life here on this earth is not linear at all—but cyclical and predictable and perpetual.

Once again, I prayed: *Please let my daughter begin to feel the power and pull of these reassuring, repetitive cycles. Let this outwardly confusing world around her begin to make sense, and show her, Lord, that the absolute surest way to move forward is by first reaching back. Whisper Your divine wisdom into her little soul, and guide her toward the realization that her ancestor's belongings are far more than mere accessories—they are, in fact, tangible, touchable family heirlooms rooted in history and steeped in symbolism.*

It was time to lift the heavy lid and lay yet another family artifact into her small, awaiting hands.

"Well, here's another little something I want to share with you. This belonged to your grandmother, too."

Slowly, carefully, I lifted the lid.

The smell of cedar circled around us, its sooty, smoky fragrance permeating the air in the room.

Leaning forward, Mary Elizabeth peered in. I wondered to myself whether the smell of cedar was filling her little heart with feelings and memories as intensely as I'd felt them an entire lifetime ago.

Instantly, upon smelling the fragrance, I visualized myself again as an infant, comfortably swaddled by my beautiful mother in my Cinderella pink baby blanket. My mind painted the picture—for perhaps the thousandth time—of Mother bending down to lay her baby girl lovingly, tenderly, into the safe confines of the large cedar drawer which had been placed on the floor just beside her writing table. I visualized Daddy carrying the drawer down the stairs—from their bedroom to our living room—then arranging the drawer "just so" in order for Mother and I to remain as close as possible while she wrote. The familiar but faraway sounds of her Underwood typewriter—*tap, tap, tap, ding!*—still fill me with inexplicable joy, and I can *still* re-create not only the *tap* but the *ding*, too! Why? Because today, Mother's typewriter sits proudly in the library of my home. The keys still hop from one to the next to create actual words on a printed page. The original bell still dings brightly when it's time to hit the carriage return and begin a new sentence. Even the space bar and the individual keys, which are worn and a bit blurry due to Mother's constant use, seem to leap with life. Looking at her typewriter transports me directly back to yesterday. I am an infant again, lying comfortably swaddled in my cedar drawer, lulled to sleep by the sounds of my mother *tap-tap-tapping* away.

With each passing minute, Mother's closeness became more palpable. I had the feeling that if I'd reached out and swiped my hand through the air around me, I would have brushed against her soft skin. My heart seemed to skip a few beats, but I settled my spirit down, determined to devote the pivotal moment completely to my little girl who sat beside me, waiting and expectant.

Reaching into our box yet again, I carefully removed a few of the items on the top layer so that I could more easily get to the layer beneath. Slowly, surely, I found what I needed, bringing it up into the brilliant light of day.

"What's that, Mom?" Mary Elizabeth asked quietly, leaning forward for closer inspection.

I unwrapped the package and carefully placed it directly into her awaiting hands.

"My mom wore this beautiful blouse on the day she was married. Hold it, honey. Feel the fabric. Try to imagine your grandmother all dressed up on her wedding day, maybe carrying a pretty bouquet of irises or lilies. What do you think?"

I watched as she lightly fingered the delicate material and I prayed that her imagination was transporting her back to that wonderful wedding day. Again, gentle, generational links were being created. Again, time lurched and tripped and galloped all over itself.

She cocked her head slightly in measured concentration, her eyes never leaving the garment that she held in her hands. I couldn't resist reaching over to brush her cheek with my fingertips.

"It's really pretty," she said quietly, still fingering the semi-sheer material lightly in her hands. "But I kind of don't get it."

The nature of her confusion confirmed for me, beyond the shadow of a doubt, that my young daughter would one day evolve into a fine, respectable memory-maker in her own right. Her questions were straightforward and completely logical.

"Why'd she wear a *blouse* on her wedding day? What'd she wear with the blouse—a skirt or something? And do you have that skirt stored away? I thought ladies wore long white gowns on their wedding day. If anybody in our family has your mom's wedding gown, it's got to be you, Mom—'cause you save just about everything you get your hands on! Why didn't you store her gown? And if you did, can I take a peek at it, just for a minute?"

I paused momentarily, slightly knocked off my center. The self-doubt began almost immediately: *Had Mother actually been married in a formal wedding gown—and if she was, where was it now? Wouldn't she have stored it away for safekeeping and passed it along to one of her six daughters? What in the Sam Hill kind of serious preservationist was I, anyway—not even knowing where my own mother's wedding gown could be found? For crying out loud!*

I knew for a fact that none of my siblings were storing the gown—but what I didn't know was whether there'd ever really been a gown at all.

Maybe Mother hadn't worn one.

Maybe she and her handsome, soon-to-be husband simply couldn't afford one.

Or, perhaps she had worn one to the ceremony, but had changed into her beautiful, puckered lavender wedding blouse immediately afterward (with a long, flowing skirt, perhaps?), for the reception.

These were riddles I couldn't solve, which momentarily toppled my spiritual equilibrium, but nudged me gently toward a critically important realization: the process of memory-making is, by no means, an exact science. It is not precise or perfect. It is not premeasured, predetermined, or formulaic. Somewhere along the way, as we pluck the memories we want to preserve, there are bound to be memory gaps and unanswerable questions. But we, as preservers of our own pasts, shouldn't allow this imprecision to frustrate us.

To the contrary. All the while—and as often as we can—we should keep digging, prodding, preserving, and packing away select pieces of our past so that the generational chains remain unbroken. Pieces will go missing. Certain stories will crisscross at illogical points. Ghosts of our past will rearrange the facts every now and then, leaving us feeling somewhat confused and disconnected. An inevitable and invariable fact: The childhood memories and recollections that we choose to pass along will occasionally fall a tiny bit short of reality. Details can become muddled and murky. Why? Because our minds are not computers; our memories are not digitized. Such gaps and omissions are unintentional.

I, myself, as a memory-maker, struggle on occasion to bat away the cobwebs and shadows that can cloud my recollections. The passage of time, combined with the porous nature of our own childhood recollections, can at times create composites of memories, creating the sensation of peering through the fragmented field of a kaleidoscope rather than the razor-sharp focus of a microscope. To a degree, it makes perfect sense that our recollections are sometimes covered in silky cobwebs that can obscure our vision and stretch our imaginations out of shape. The memories we choose to preserve and retrieve—as frustrating as they may be—often resemble a string of last year's Christmas tree lights: difficult to untangle, but beautifully illuminating nonetheless.

Even as I recall some of the details within the shared stories of this book, I know that my memory bank is not airtight and ironclad. No one's is. But as memory-makers, we must not despair. The past still calls, and we must still answer.

In that same vein, I am careful not to position myself among my beautiful siblings as the sole keeper of the flame (but I am the primary "keeper," they'd all agree). I don't possess every last bauble. As memory-makers, my siblings and I are responsible like that; each of us has within our possession precious items and heirlooms that link us to our collective past; things we can hold in our hands and remember our parents by, in our own special, unique ways. No, my Forever Box is by no means the official or sole repository for all this familial history.

That would be selfish.

I don't possess every single last piece of my grandmother's twelve-piece dinner setting (in fact, I don't have *any*). I believe there are only a few settings left—and even those are incomplete.

But they do exist.

❧

OTHER belongings of Mama Lilly's exist as well: a beautiful Tiffany lamp and an ornate china cabinet sit proudly in my sister Noelle's beautiful home. Also in Noelle's home: a very large, dark, and stunning oil portrait of Mother in her mid-twenties, her delicate hands resting comfortably in her lap and her eyes cast downward in contemplation. I am relieved and proud to know that, among us, we spread the memories around, and we share our pieces freely. There's no such thing as a greedy memory-maker. The very nature of the process itself begs for physical and spiritual collaboration.

Mary Elizabeth and I both gazed at the blouse again, letting our imaginations wander back to that glorious wedding day. The blouse is lavender in color, delicate as a piece of antique lace, with puckered rows of material carefully sewn across the front. At the right shoulder, there are five tiny silver eyehooks, which gently close the blouse at the neck. Two more silver hooks at the waist. (Unfortunately, the blouse is slightly torn at the upper right shoulder, but all else about the garment remains perfectly intact.)

It's clear that the garment had, indeed, been handmade, because the stitching along the neckline is slightly askew in some places, and the eyehooks are a tiny bit misaligned. I love to hold the garment in my hands, because every time I do, I visualize Mother in the quiet evenings just before her wedding, threading her needle by the soft and dimming lamplight, carefully creating the blouse that would escort her into an exciting, new life as Mrs. James W. Clark.

"She sure did sew well!" Mary Elizabeth observed, taking an important, figurative step closer to her maternal grandmother.

"She was an expert," I said proudly. "She even made some of our coats, dresses, and skirts. Your grandmother was as good a seamstress as I've ever seen."

The scenes of their wedding day were still dancing around in my mind. I could see Mother: perfect, petite, and infinitely proud to be standing beside my father, her dashing new husband. Maybe my father was holding her hand. When they were pronounced husband and wife, perhaps they came together, momentarily, for a tender kiss and gentle embrace. I could see from my daughter's facial expression that she'd been pulled in by the powerful images as well, mesmerized by the magic of the moment.

When it was time to return Mother's blouse to the box, it was Mary Elizabeth who folded it, wrapped it, and carefully placed it back into the shadowed confines.

❧

WHEN Mary Elizabeth was a mere toddler, dancing was one of her greatest joys. By age four, we'd enrolled her in her first dance class.

She was blissful, obviously very much in her element.

As soon as the curtain came down on her very first end-of-the-year dance recital, we started making memories and continuing family traditions. Another pivotal moment presented itself: It was Mary Elizabeth's first time depositing one of her own personal and prized possessions into the Forever Box.

Quite the ceremony.

What we were preserving were her first pair of tiny ballet slippers; the same ones she'd worn during that first recital. On the bottom of the tiny leather soles, in dark blue ink, I'd carefully inscribed the details: "Mary Elizabeth's First Ballet Slippers, September 1993." Guiding her tiny, toddler-size hands (she was about four), I instructed my daughter on how to properly wrap the slippers in tissue paper then insert them into the ever-reliable, airtight zippered pouch.

Since that magical afternoon and over the span of her lifetime—even throughout her college days—Mary Elizabeth evolved into a serious student of classical ballet and modern dance. To visually capture my daughter's steady and sure progression as a dancer, one simple preservation technique proved highly effective.

Every several years, usually right after a recital (which always signaled the end of yet another year of dancing), she'd enter the slippers into the darkened confines of the box. To visually emphasize the passage of time throughout her years as a dancer, we placed each successive pair of slippers into the same bag, alongside the tiny pair from her very first ballet recital as a four-year-old.

Today, when she reaches into the box to bring her slippers into the brilliant light of day, she can more fully appreciate the fact that dance has indeed played a vital role in her life over and throughout her lifetime, from toddler to adult. I am enormously grateful that we thought to save them. Why? Because, along with the shared verbal history surrounding those years, they tell her dancing story by providing tactile proof of the passage of time; the passage of a lifetime, in fact. Passages that she, eventually, will share with her own daughters, and eventually her granddaughters, and the story will continue long after I am gone.

So the cycle dances merrily along.

❧

It is no coincidence that I, too, loved dance with the same passion and fury as Mary Elizabeth, beginning at about the age of five or six. To this very day, my memories of dance, particularly as it concerned dance with Mother, remain crystal clear and miraculously distinct. I remember very well the hot, hazy afternoon that I witnessed, for the first time in my little life, the sight of professional dancers moving across a stage. They were perfect. Precise. Powerful. And they had bronzed-brown skin, just like me!

It was a defining moment in my young life.

There we were, mother and daughter, sitting together in the darkened performance hall of Detroit's beautiful (and historic) Fisher Building. Mother had splurged on two tickets to see the Alvin Ailey American Dance Theater, and the seats were great.

I will never forget it.

I was short, so my feet didn't touch the floor as I pushed my little bottom all the way to the back of my seat. I was mesmerized. Involuntarily, as I watched those dancers leap and glide across the stage, my body jumped a tiny bit this way and jerked a tiny bit that way; I was moving right along with them as they flew through the air with such soul and grace that it took my breath away.

I remember the feel of the chair's soft velvet against the backs of my legs and the hush that quieted the entire audience as the house lights dimmed and the curtain lifted. By the time the company reached their final, signature piece, "Revelations," I was crying happy, wholesome tears. I'd never ever experienced anything so physically precise and emotionally evocative—and my youthful tears just wouldn't stop flowing.

Mother allowed me to cry.

To this day, I remain steeped in gratitude toward my mom for simply allowing me the luxury of sitting through my own tears. Somehow, she knew instinctively that any interruption—from her or anybody else—would have diluted the power and intensity of this deeply personal experience. So what did she do? She let me be. She allowed my tears to flow that afternoon as we sat in that darkened theater. Mother simply knew, deep within that secret place nestled in her maternal soul, that her baby girl was experiencing, for the very first time in her young life, the power of witnessing art in its purest forms. The movement, music, and choreography threatened to stop my little heart. And as I watched them fly—those miraculous dancers who looked just like me—I somehow knew I'd never be the same again.

A part of my soul had opened up.

It took me decades to realize this, but Mother realized and appreciated my need to absorb that powerful experience in its totality, without interruption. After a few minutes, though, and to my great relief, she did reach over and grasp my hand.

During intermission, we filed slowly out with the crowd. Mother bought me a box of Milk Duds. ("Eat that candy out here," she whispered urgently, "because you're certainly not bringing that melting chocolate back into the theater with you!") At the conclusion of the performance, we filed out again with the dispersing crowd, emerging from the darkened theater into the Fisher's grand lobby and the brilliant light of day. Mother gazed down at me with a soft smile, something very close to sympathy in her eyes. She leaned down close to my little cheeks and gently kissed away the tracks of my recent tears. (She never wiped; almost always kissed.)

As we were riding home that afternoon, I remember feeling like some new layer of awareness had just gently washed over my spirit. This was a paper-thin layer of deepened enlightenment; thin as the skin of an onion and light as a fleeing thought. Something fresh and wonderfully invigorating had begun dancing a little jig in my soul. I realize now that it might have been my first youthful experience with spiritual enlightenment. Watching those dancers had completely removed me from myself, lifting me far above the finite little details of my own personal circumstances. That afternoon, the power and glory of dance, as a pure and powerful art form, insinuated itself into my spirit—and here it remains to this day.

So thank you, sweet Mother. *Thank you for opening up my soul.*

How blessed I am to have passed this passion to yet another emerging generation. The memories and the mother-daughter traditions remain comfortably embedded in our lives.

And even though Mother is gone, her passionate soul and her spiritual generosity will live forever.

ℭϿ

TODAY, taking my place in the proud line of preservationists, it should come as no surprise that my daughter and I make it a point to see the Ailey dancers every year, thereby continuing the mother-daughter tradition that my own mother began with me, decades ago. It is a highlight of our mother-daughter experience.

Each time, just before the performance, the two of us, now adult women, enjoy dinner—during which we pray, laugh, love—and remember that miraculous woman who was my mother. I describe to my baby girl, on a consistent basis, those vivid childhood recollections with my mom during that magical afternoon at the Fisher. Of how I sat in that soft velvet chair, joyous tears streaming down my face.

So it is with a sense of historical knowledge and generational continuity that, during every Ailey performance, I manage to sneak several sidelong glances at my daughter as she watches the dancers leap across the stage. Why? To witness, up close and personally, the myriad of emotions that shadow her face as the company performs. Yes, she's already promised that when (and if) she has a daughter of her own, the Ailey dancers will become a regular part of their cultural life as well. So the tradition continues, mother to daughter; mother to daughter. That comfortably repetitive cycle of life that defines the concept of forever.

❧

WHEN Lonnie Paul and Mary Elizabeth were in grade school, my husband, Lonnie, and I took them on safari throughout

Kenya. We were led by a miracle of a man, himself a revered Masai warrior, who'd come to the United States to further his education. Fortunately for our family, Joseph began teaching social studies at my children's middle school, and a close relationship was quickly forged. It was Joseph, who was well-loved and well-respected in his native country, who led us on a pilgrimage home. With Joseph at the helm, we traveled back to our ancestral homeland. Traveling with a small group of others, my family came to know firsthand the kind, beautiful people of Kenya and the country's breathtakingly beautiful physical terrain.

Our days were spent traveling deep into the bush, watching as God's creatures moved freely about in their natural habitat. A pair of graceful giraffes bending down to nibble the succulent leaves from the tops of an acacia tree. The lazy leopard, napping on the branch of a tree only a few feet above us, its tail dangling so close we could almost reach up and give it a soft yank. During the evenings in particular, the Masai warriors came in close around us. They built great bonfires, giant red-orange embers popping and crackling into the thick dark of night. The warriors cooked us feasts every night, and laughed with us well into every evening.

On one of these magical evenings in Kenya, my mind traveled back to the childhood memory of me and my grandmother sitting together in her living room. I smiled as I remembered how excited she'd been to share with me the details of her own trip to Africa. I thought about the leather purse she'd brought back for me from Cairo, and the pride I could hear in her voice as she talked about the dawn of civilization beginning on the very continent where I happened to be standing at that moment. I invited the powerful pull of these intertwining moments to shower over me, feeling the gentle presence of generational continuity wrap itself around my shoulders, as well as a newly heightened sense of self-awareness and ancestral pride.

God's presence moved somewhere deep in my spirit.

Fighting tears, I moved closer in toward my family as we stood before that raging Kenyan bonfire. I relished their comforting presence and tried mightily to preserve the magic of that special moment. Together, our little group gazed up at the stars; tiny pricks of shining light painted in a black velvet sky. The low-hanging Kenyan moon illuminated my children's faces with light almost as bright as the sun. They, too, stood in quiet awe.

Leaning in close to my son, I whispered softly: "Try your hardest to remember this moment forever. Think about it every day, if only for a moment, so that your memory of *right now* remains fresh in your mind."

He nodded, silent.

"Promise me?" I implored, fighting the suddenly desperate desire to cover his face in kisses. (Such a maternal display of physical affection would have embarrassed him to no end—*especially* in the revered presence of the mighty Masai warriors who stood with us, robed and regal, under the stars.)

"I promise, Mom. I'll do my best," he answered, sounding doubtful but deliberate at the same time.

"That's all I can ask, beautiful boy . . . That you try."

It was important to me that my children exercised and challenged their minds on a constant basis, not only to enhance their mental acuity but to strengthen their spiritual condition as well. Something as simple as preserving a specific memory—if only by *reflecting on it* each day—was an easy exercise that would (and did) massage and strengthen their emotional clarity. It taught them, from an early age, how to catalog special moments. In short, it taught them how to *memorialize* memories.

೮ு

So the ever-widening patterns continue, like a stone dropped in the middle of a pond.

Let each and every one of us take up our role as memory-keepers, resolving individually and collectively to keep our "centers" intact and well-preserved.

And, no matter whether you believe in God or Jesus or a Higher Power or a Supreme Being—whatever your spiritual/religious beliefs—let us grow stronger by pulling our pasts around our shoulders. Let us give powerful and profound thanks to whatever Power is greater than us, and ask that we be led and guided, as conscientious memory-keepers, so that our legacies will live on long, long after we take our leave of this earthly place.

BY MARY ELIZABETH TAYLOR

SANKOFA

———— ❦ ————

Our time on this earth is finite. Each lifetime has a defined measurement. No, there is no crystal ball that can predict the precise moment our individual lives will come to a close, but this much is certain: We move about the world subconsciously aware that ours is a mortal, momentary existence. Life is fleeting and mercurial. Slippery and exhaustible. Utterly impossible to hold on to forever, although many of us might very well want to (thankfully, not me).

This much is sure: None of us can escape the eventual and inevitable clutches of death, but what we can control is the quality and significance of those cherished belongings we purposefully choose to leave behind. As the old adage goes, "You can't take it with you." My response to that has always been, *Who would even want to?* No matter what your religious or spiritual convictions, I think it is safe to say that many, if not most, of us can agree that when our lives finally come to a close, the earthly things we so cherish—even covet—won't be coming along for our ride. (Hence, the rhetorical question, *Ever figure out why you never see a moving van at a funeral?*)

Put simply, by exercising care and deliberation while we're here on this earth, we can almost leapfrog over the snapping clutches of death by preserving *vital pieces not only from our past, but from our present-day lives as well, pieces that can be mulled over and turned around and softly touched by the loved ones who live on long after we leave. When we leave behind for our children not only the ability* but the desire to weave their past, present, and future into one whole cloth, we're leaving for them invaluable spiritual road maps that will lead them and guide them as they struggle to negotiate the turbulent, topsy-turvy world around them. We should teach them to cherish and care for the items that are special to them, with a keen eye trained always toward the permanence of preservation. They need to know how to draw strength and sustenance not only from the magnetic pull of the past, but also from the power of the present and the promise of the future. They need to know, in their mind and heart and spirit, that these three things—the past, the present, and the future—can, and do, comfortably coexist. This three-pronged approach will enrich their lives and add depth and meaning to their daily existence. I am totally convinced that the most lasting and loving gift we can leave our progeny is the clear understanding that, in order for them to move forward in the world, they must be rooted (but not stuck) in the past, grateful for and cognizant of the present, and warmly welcoming of the future.

The West African concept of Sankofa encapsulates this principle perfectly. One of the images of this ancient concept is the Sankofa Bird, symbolic in spirit and magically mythic, who flies forward while continually looking back (while holding an egg in its mouth, which symbolizes the future). By doing so, he reminds us that in order to truly achieve our fullest potential as we move forward in our lives, we must reach back to gather the best of what our past has to teach us. It's an enlightened, holistic concept to be sure, and certainly a principle that each and every one of us can put to practical use.

I love the Sankofa Bird because it speaks directly to my spirit. I love that as he flies across his own brilliant blue sky, he's reminding each of us that whatever we think we have lost, we can find again; that whatever we think we've long since forgotten can be deliberately reclaimed, and that our lives can be spiritually revived, emotionally enriched, and physically reenergized when we make the deliberate attempt to piece together our past and preserve the most positive parts of our present.

It is this concept that I invite you to embrace by putting it into effect in your own daily life.

As you begin your personal journey toward becoming a more conscientious memory-maker, here are a few tips on how best to preserve the brightest pieces (and wisest principles) in your own lives. I offer up these tips as little bits of love. I pray that you not only receive them as acts of spiritual kindness, but that you try mightily to incorporate them into your daily routine. And here I make a personal promise: When you put some (or all) of these suggestions into practice, you'll find that, over time, your life will simply *open itself up*, like a delicate red rose or a bright purple morning glory. You'll begin to feel more consciously connected to the universe around you as your life expands far beyond itself—far beyond the earthly time constraints that define us as mere mortals.

Over time, I've found that these suggestions have worked for me. Unfortunately, I don't follow every last recommendation as precisely as I should. I can be a bit careless sometimes, or irregular with my "entries." None of us are perfect. As we move forward with the intricacies of this preservation process, we must remember that memory-making is a highly personalized experience. There is no one right way to do it.

The process should not feel formulaic, but free-flowing

and fun, never forced. As you begin your memory-making journey, know with certainty that there are no rigid, preexisting sets of rules or binding criteria you must follow to make this process work. Never take the process too seriously. Only *you* can determine which items are significant enough to preserve and insert into your Forever Box. The beauty of this process is that it's deeply personal. These memories are *yours*—no one else's. So how, when, and why you decide to pluck certain pieces of your past is strictly and solely up to you! Have fun!

Listen Closely. Teach yourself to listen *actively*. To do this, you must clear your mind of all else—namely, your own personal circumstances—so that you not only hear but *understand* the memories, ideas, and life lessons that your friends and loved ones share with you. Remember, they are entrusting you not only to preserve and pass along their sentiments and stories, but to validate the fact that they even existed on this earth at all and that their lives counted for something significant and pleasing.

To become a better memory-maker, seek out the senior family members and friends who've been important in your life. Ask them questions about their past, and mindfully visualize their answers so that you can fit them comfortably, consciously, into your own psyche. Weave their wisdom into the fabric of your own life. To more effectively preserve the clarity of their shared memories, consider taping your conversations. (I regret not having done this myself.) Video is the best way to preserve simultaneously both the physical image *and* the verbal account.

Another important tip as you sit down with your senior friends and family: Be prepared! Map out your questions beforehand, and jot them down. And when dealing with seniors, always treat them with the dignity and respect they deserve. (When asking questions of them, speak clearly, succinctly, and loudly enough for elderly people to comfortably hear you. Never yell or gesticulate wildly in the mistaken belief that they might understand you more clearly.)

Here are some questions to consider as you begin these crucial steps toward becoming a plucker of memories:

- In what year were you born?

- Where did you grow up?

- How many siblings/children/grandchildren did/do you have?

- What were the names of two or three of your closest childhood friends?

- What did you do for fun?

- Can you describe your childhood home and community?

- What are a few of the brightest, most brilliant memories from your youth?

- Would you show me, or consider passing along to me for safekeeping, any mementos/objects from your past, and describe their history and significance?

Keep It Simple. Both literally and figuratively, keep the process simple. My Forever Box happens to be cedar. Why cedar? Because I love its smoky smell as well as the childhood memories its mere aroma evokes. Because of the natural preservative quality of the wood itself. Most important, because cedar is a comfortable medium for *me*. To create your own repository, select something that's comfortable and manageable *for you*—whether it's a cardboard box, a wicker basket, or a more elaborate, durable hope chest. Remember that it's not the box itself, *but the memories inside the box that count.*

Your ability to keep the process simple assures that you will also, hopefully, keep the process filled with fun. Don't take it so seriously that it becomes a stressor in your life. Go with the flow. Trust your instincts. Avoid using complicated charts, graphs, and overly detailed chronologies. You're not looking to become a professional historian; you simply want to learn to become a comfortably conscientious memory-maker.

Select the items that you want to preserve with great care, and try to develop a heightened sense of discernment.

By this I mean avoid placing any and every "first" item into your box (avoid that "first science fair project" and the "first laptop computer" as well as that "first house of toothpicks that little Bobby made in second grade"). The preservation process itself mandates that you work within a confined amount of space. Surprisingly, this physical limitation is actually a good thing. Why? Because working within a specific and predetermined amount of space will strengthen your selectivity skills.

A few questions to ask concerning simplicity as you begin to build your Forever Box:

- Am I being careful to include not only the old items (preserving history), but the items from my present-day life as well (creating new memories)?

- Am I becoming overly anxious about what, when, why, and how to collect?

- Is the entire process of my memory-making becoming too complicated and involved, to the point where it's distracting? *Am I having fun?*

Handle with Care. When storing fabric or material, wrap the item first in several layers of tissue paper, being careful to insert tissue paper between every layer of fabric. Fold the item carefully, then store in a plastic bag. (Zipper-sealing bags work fine. For larger items, the clear plastic covering from your dry cleaner works well, too.)

Avoid preserving bulky items such as heavy clothing and thick garments. Rather than packing away Aunt Matilda's entire mohair coat, for example, simply snip a few small pieces of the inner and outer lining instead. Take a photo of the coat, then insert the photo into the bag as well. This way you're able to preserve and pass along not only the feel of the actual material, but you'll be able to enjoy the visual image, too.

Any delicate ornaments such as glass or crystal should first be wrapped in tissue paper, then covered in bubble wrap. If you have the space, try to stack your delicate items in their own separate section, dividing each artifact with solid cardboard to create a safety buffer between each piece. Ideally, whichever repository you select should have a lid or protective cover of some kind (this is why baskets don't always work), not only to protect the contents from sunlight but also to minimize the risk of damage if the box is accidentally dropped or suddenly jarred.

Keep your Forever Box in a cool, shady location. Be aware that direct and sustained sunlight fades and even disintegrates photosensitive chemicals in fabrics, newsprint, and photographs. Also consider using acid-free sleeves and envelopes for these items, which should help retard the aging process considerably.

Once you've selected a location for your box, if at all possible, make it permanent. Constant rearrangement of your repository unsettles the contents inside and gets you out of the habit of retreating to one safe, predetermined location when it's time to make an entry.

Label and date each item. This doesn't have to be a complicated process: even using a sticky note will do—just as long as each item is somehow cataloged.

VERY IMPORTANT: When entering, removing, or sharing the items in your box, *make sure your hands are completely clean and dry.* Never *ever* use hand lotions or creams before handling pieces. (The perspiration and natural oils from your skin will create stains, smudges, and fingerprints, particularly on leather items or extremely aged and delicate fabrics.)

Finally, don't be afraid of mothballs! Many new brands have been developed that are without any scent at all. What wonderful news: Your Forever Box doesn't *have* to smell like your grandmother's closet after all!

Some questions to ask yourself as you prepare to focus on safe handling:

- Is my box in a location that is convenient and comfortable for me?

- Are the pieces inside strategically placed and carefully wrapped?

- Have I remembered to catalog and/or date each item so that its significance will not fade over time?

- Have I politely requested that everyone participating in the memory-making process keep their hands clean and lotion-free?

Create a Quiet Sanctuary. Whenever you open your Forever Box—whether it's to insert a new piece or retrieve an old one—try to create a peaceful, tranquil environment. It needn't be overly ceremonial. Remember, though, that you're not simply tossing your pieces into a junk drawer or random box; you're reflecting on the memories, stories, and principles *behind* these baubles, and this process requires a heightened sense of inner calm and serenity.

To create a peaceful buffer from the noisy, clanging world around you, disconnect all things electronic. Shut the door on anything that buzzes, beeps, or brings stress or angst into your spirit—at least for these brief but vital memory-making moments. More than anything, know that *true* inner peace comes to us more easily when our souls are still. In the silence of our words, our Higher Power will speak.

Some questions as you prepare to still your spirit and seek tranquility:

- Is my soul as calm as it can be? Can I actually *feel* my heart rate slowing and my pulse slowing to a more relaxed level?

- Have I quieted my mind and emptied it completely of the day's frenzied, frantic activity, so much so that my thoughts are no longer racing and my stress has slowed to a virtual standstill?

- Have I tried deep breathing, prayer, meditation, tai chi, yoga, or herbal tea to bring about a calmer, more contemplative aura?

- Have I made enough emotional/spiritual space in my mind so that I can now invite the memories to come flowing in?

Share Your Skills with Others. When capturing the pieces of your past, try not to do it alone. Bring others along for the ride! Enlist the help of the young people around you, and teach them what you've learned so far about the importance of handling items properly, in a respectful, non-chaotic environment. Invite the senior friends and family members in your life to participate in the process as well. Perhaps they can even add a few of their own prized possessions to the box, while sharing the stories behind their pieces. This is not only a warm and wonderful way to validate a senior's sense of importance and significance, but it's also facilitates and nurtures the long-lost art of multigenerational bonding and stimulates meaningful, intergenerational communication.

Also try to make contact with other memory-makers to compare notes on what works best and what doesn't. Pull together an informal group of friends who might be interested in starting the process *together*—much like the quilting bees of yesterday. Although I don't do this myself, consider reaching out to others (even strangers—they have good ideas, too!) by posting and comparing notes on the Internet or even beginning your own memory-making website so that others can become a collective part of this exciting, collaborative process. Don't operate in isolation. This process is much too precious *not* to share with others!

Questions that will encourage you to reach out to others for ideas, fellowship, and fun:

- Do I actively solicit ideas and advice from other memory-makers?

- Have I been patient with and kind to my relatives/ friends as I enlist their assistance with my memory-making?

- If I were to die tomorrow, could I leave this earth confident in the knowledge that I've passed along the necessary memory-making skills to my loved ones so that my living legacy continues?

The next step: Simply sit back and enjoy. Invite your life to open up around you.

You are a collector now.

And it is your baubles, your beliefs, and the rewoven bits

of the most pleasing parts of your past that will bring sustenance, spiritual depth, and emotional solidity to the rest of your living days . . . and beyond.

As you live your daily life, fly like the Sankofa Bird. Propel yourself forward while looking back. Live in the moment, but keep an eye trained toward the future. Pull your past around you and seek comfort in its solidity.

And when all of these converge, your soul can smile a wide, warm smile . . . because you will have finally learned how to create *forever*.

Questions for Discussion

———————— ∞ ————————

1. In order to re-create poignant childhood memories, the author relies on every one of her five senses—sight, hearing, smell, taste, and touch—to take the reader on a journey into her past. For example, she chooses a cedar chest for her Forever Box because the smell of cedar evokes such powerfully positive emotions within her. Digging deep into your memory, try to recall a particularly powerful scent, sight, or sound from your youth that can still—even today—transport you immediately back to your childhood. What is it? What feelings does it elicit?

2. Reflect on the people who influenced you most profoundly during your childhood. Why were they

important? What did they leave behind that continues to live on through you?

3. A recurring theme in *The Forever Box* is the power and beauty of lasting, durable friendships among women. Do you make the conscientious effort to cherish and celebrate the close friends in your life, or does the "I'm too busy right now" syndrome get in the way of your efforts? What steps can you take to maintain and nurture the close friendships you enjoy in your life?

4. In passing down her precious church hat, the author's mother also passes along several important life lessons about maintaining dignity in the face of adversity and grace under pressure. What larger lessons do you hope to share with the young people in your life, in hopes that they, too, will one day pass along to future generations?

5. The three-pronged approach to leading a satisfying, meaningful life is a constant theme throughout *The Forever Box* (that is, fearlessly embracing the future, mindfully living in the present day, and preserving the most positive pieces of our past). Would adopting this three-pronged approach add more balance to your life? What steps do you need to take in your own life to achieve the three-pronged vision?

6. It's clear that the author is powerfully drawn to all things that are old—whether it's her close relationships with the four elderly women in her life, or with the actual treasures that they share with her. Reflect on your own relationships with the seniors in your life. Do you make the effort to glean their wisdom, listen to their stories, and celebrate their existence?

7. Mrs. Simpson shares with the young Kristin not only her teacups and scratch biscuits, but her heightened spiritual awareness as well, an awareness that is the centering force of the author's life today. Reflect on not just the baubles but the *beliefs and principles* that were passed down to you by earlier generations. What are they? Have you successfully incorporated these principles into your daily life? How will you pass these principles down to future generations?

8. Why was the author's visit with Miss Miriam so transformative and powerful? Why were Miss Miriam's progressive views on women so relevant?

9. Not every element of our collective, historical past is positive. How are the painful pieces of our past treated in this book? (For example, the ravages of slavery and the horrors of the Holocaust.) Do you agree or disagree with the author's assertion that it's vital to pass

along historical knowledge to successive generations—even if the lessons are painful?

10. Are you ready to become a more conscientious memory-maker in your own right? What ideas come to mind as you consider starting your own Forever Box?

11. Reflect on the pieces of the past that you may already have. What are they, and who passed them along to you? What was—and is—their significance in your life?

12. Are you confident that your treasures and beliefs will remain alive long after you're gone? Have you decided on the people in your life who will be your memory-keepers?

13. Beyond creating lasting remnants of earlier times, what else does *The Forever Box* seek to preserve?